EQUALITY IS BIBLICAL

Pen Wilcock, a writer, thinker and teacher, has worked in school, hospice and prison chaplaincy contexts and as the pastor of a number of Methodist churches. She lives in Hastings (in England's East Sussex) where she is a Local Preacher in the Methodist circuit. You can find her online at her blog *Kindred of the Quiet Way*.

'There is no hierarchy of the sexes in the Bible's creation stories. The image of God is universalised. The whole of humankind – every woman as well as every man – shares equally in the responsibility and privilege of being representatives of their creator. The language is deliberate. God's voice undermines the social structure of an ancient world laden with oppressive sexism and violence. This was nothing short of a revolution. It is just as revolutionary today, because as you explore the rest of the biblical record and Church history – not to mention the values of our contemporary society – this foundational principle has long been neglected and even lost. That is why I whole-heartedly recommend Pen Wilcock's eye opening, thought provoking and paradigm shifting book as an agenda for humanity.'
Steve Chalke, Founder and Leader of Oasis Global

'A fresh and very helpful look at the issue of equality for the everyday Christian. Pen skilfully takes us through some complex theology at a pace that allows us to dig deep and make some important decisions for ourselves.'
Tola Fisher, Editor of *Woman Alive*

'This book digs deep into the roots of equality. With an uncanny ability to curate and communicate information, Penelope grapples with the issues and then helps you to reflect on them for yourself. Providing historical and biblical examples to have at your fingertips, this book will be a great tool in your toolkit as you consider again the importance of equality for all people. A fascinating read.'
Cathy Madavan, speaker, author and board member of the Kyria Network

Also by Penelope Wilcock

FICTION

The Hawk and the Dove (Lion Hudson)

The Wounds of God (Lion Hudson)

The Long Fall (Lion Hudson)

The Hardest Thing to Do (Lion Hudson)

The Hour Before Dawn (Lion Hudson)

Remember Me (Lion Hudson)

The Breath of Peace (Lion Hudson)

The Beautiful Thread (Lion Hudson)

A Day and a Life (Lion Hudson)

The Clear Light of Day (David C. Cook)

Thereby Hangs A Tale (Kingsway)

NON-FICTION

In Celebration of Simplicity (Lion Hudson)

The Road of Blessing (Lion Hudson)

Learning to Let Go (Lion Hudson)

Spiritual Care of Dying and Bereaved People (BRF)

Equality Is Biblical (SPCK)

Into the Heart of Advent (SPCK)

RESOURCE BOOKS

100 Stand-Alone Bible Studies (Lion Hudson)

100 More Stand-Alone Bible Studies (Lion Hudson)

The Wilderness Within You (Lion Hudson)

52 Original Wisdom Stories (Lion Hudson)

POETRY

Urban Angel (with Stewart Henderson and Ben Ecclestone; Piquant)

EQUALITY IS BIBLICAL

Lifting the curse of Eve

Penelope Wilcock

First published in Great Britain in 2020

Society for Promoting Christian Knowledge
36 Causton Street
London SW1P 4ST
www.spck.org.uk

British Library Cataloguing-in-Publication Data
A catalogue record for this book is available from the British Library

ISBN 978–0–281–08300–8
eBook ISBN 978–0–281–08301–5

Typeset by Nord Compo
First printed in Great Britain by Jellyfish Print Solutions

eBook by by Nord Compo

Produced on paper from sustainable forests

Contents

Contents

Acknowledgments

My thanks to Graham and Val Hamer for bringing their scholarship to a meticulous reading of my text. Their comments were full of insight and intelligence and helped greatly.

A note to the reader

My father's approach to snacks was a great trial to my mother.

I was born in the second half of the 1950s, when pre-lunch and pre-dinner drinks were a definite thing. On any Sunday morning at our parish church, invitations would be quietly shared in discreet tones to come over for drinks before lunch – and in the evening while supper was still finishing off in the oven, my parents would sit down for a sherry before they moved to the (immaculately laid) dining table to eat. Ha! People did things properly back then! None of this propping one's enamel dish upon an accumulation of midriff fat to shovel down spag bol while watching the telly.

The preprandial drinks had accompanying snacks, as did coffee at elevenses and tea in the late afternoon. And these were the bone of contention.

My father, offered salted peanuts with his sherry, would grab a handful, cup them in his palm, toss them carelessly into his mouth – crunch, crunch, swallow. Likewise if my mother offered him a biscuit[1]. He'd shove it into his mouth whole, munch rapidly and swallow. Or orange juice might appear on the menu instead of sherry. In the 1960s, stores boasted no extensive ranges of every kind of fruit juice temptingly displayed in chilled cabinets. No. It came in tins, and you purchased it for special occasions. My father would take up the diminutive glass with the precious tinned orange juice and knock it back in about three consecutive glugs.

My mother, eating her peanuts one by one or taking tiny bites of

---

1   US reader, I don't mean what you mean by 'biscuit'. Not a hearty thing you eat with gravy that we in the UK call a scone. I mean a dainty, crisp, small, flat cookie that breaks with a snap – more like a communion wafer than like a bread roll.

her crispy biscuit, would watch in furious disbelief. 'You're supposed to savour it, Steve! You don't even taste it! What's the point?'

But she never changed him, partly because he enjoyed baiting her. He liked saying the simple word 'dandelion' (he was chief weeder of our garden) not as DAN-de-lion like everybody else, but as dan-DAY-lee-on, because he knew it irritated her. Annoying my mother was an entertainment that never grew old for him.

But how about you? When it comes to snacks are you a nibbler or a gobbler? And what about when it comes to books? This particular book is only snack-sized – not one of your weighty hundred-thou-sand-word tomes. Is your plan to consume it in one bite because it's short? Reader, I beg you not to. Try to go mindfully enough to read the footnotes, and take the time to look up the Bible passages. Check out the work of Marg Mowczko and Peter Selby. At least, at the end of each chapter, will you pause and reflect as I shall invite you to do? Ask yourself, 'What does this mean, in *my* life?' Let the thoughts soak in; give them the chance to provoke ideas of your own, and turn those over in your mind as they rise to the surface. This book, like life itself, is only brief, but let us savour our time together. And if you want to reply, if you have comments of your own, you can write to me via my publisher or find me online at *Kindred of the Quiet Way*.[2] This book is written for you, not for me – and I offer it for you to really savour and enjoy. Not crunch-crunch-swallow. Please.

---

2   <https://kindredofthequietway.blogspot.com>

1

Sources of wisdom and authority

The personal responsibility
of exploration

Keep looking. Keep listening. Never stop wondering, asking questions, challenging what you already believe.

Back in the 1980s, I had a friend, a middle-aged man, with aspirations to leadership within the Methodist Church tradition. Gifted and inspirational, others encouraged him to follow the Methodist route to church leadership and train as a Local Preacher. He wouldn't. Why? In his youth he'd known someone who took this path and encountered strong challenges to cherished beliefs. The result? That young man concluded he had been duped and mistaken, and he abandoned the Christian way; it wasn't true after all. He fell into the all-or-nothing trap, and so did my friend. Horrified by that long-ago experience of seeing someone lose their faith, he strove to protect the delicate flower of his own conviction against the frosts and winds and scorching sun of this wild world. He built a greenhouse around it and kept it there, nourished by packet fertilizers and water from the tap. He simply refused the concept that faith is a wild flower able to put down roots in the crevices of the highest crag or the rich earth of impenetrable forests. Faith can be blasted by adversity and debate and personal honesty – but it rises again, for the simple reason that God is really there and the gospel is really true and Christ waits for us to notice him and take his living Way. There is much in this world to make us afraid, but one thing we don't need to be scared of is the unwelcome discovery that the gospel was only a fairy tale – because it's not.

The snake has a bad press in Christian tradition, but we can learn even from the much-reviled serpent! Its old skin gets tight. It out-grows it. So it makes the effort to squeeze out of that confinement, to escape the constriction of what no longer fits, and move on. And so should we.

This book is only short. I like short books. I am no great theologian; I haven't spent my life poring over the tomes of difficult theology. My own way has been somewhat more feral and marginal than that, wandering along, asking 'What if?' I love the Scriptures, and they have quenched the thirst of my soul since I was a child. But I like the fresh water that trickles unexpected from the rock, not the sort that comes in plastic bottles which they charge you money for. 'How blessed are those who, taking the lonely hike through the grim landscape of Death Valley, find it to be a place of springs.'[1] And even though the book is short, I felt it had to be written – it came out of an experience that momentarily caused my jaw to drop.

I thought, you see, that all Christians were searchers and seek-ers – tracking the wild Lion through paths sometimes hard to fol-low. I used to write Bible notes for a publisher who resources the faith community with daily devotional study, and they asked me for a set of notes about women in the New Testament. The copy I sent them included (in the merest of brief paragraphs – Bible notes aren't long) allusion to the thesis of this book: that the healing work of the Cross includes the restoration of gender equality, and that Church history shows we have ignored this aspect of Christ's work for far too long. To my astonishment, the publisher took issue with my assertion. 'But I can demonstrate it is true,' I said. And then came the death blow to our professional relationship. They replied that it might be true but that, regardless of what is *true*, my job as a writer and theirs as a publisher was to reassure their readers by supplying them *with what they already believed*. We were not in the business of challenging established understanding. We were

---

1 Psalms 84.6, my paraphrase.

patching the greenhouse, not going out into the mountains to look for wildflowers.

This is what can be thought of as marketplace-led theology, and it stinks. That publisher and I parted company, but I still wanted to share with you what they wouldn't let me say in those Bible notes. So here is my little book, which proposes to you an understanding about gender equality rooted in the Scripture but flowering and fruiting in the living practice of our everyday faith. Because, for goodness sake, we must have courage in this journey. We must be able to stand like Elijah at the mouth of the cave, like Abraham interceding for the city, in the face of the living God, and ask him, 'But what about this? What did you mean? Where is it leading? What path is there for my feet to find *today*?'

In his book *Miracles*, C.S. Lewis famously proposed two options for wise discipleship: either to obey the received tradition without question, or to be prepared to undertake the struggle for true insight and Christian scholarship ourselves. He offered the view that either the adventure of authentic exploration or the security of relying on ancient wisdom would equally serve us. He said we had to either go on or go back, but it would be death to just stay where we are.

I almost agree with him, except for one thing. I think to go back is death as well. I don't believe any of us on the way of faith is offered the luxury of going back. As Jesus put it, 'No one who puts his hand to the plow and looks back is fit for the kingdom of God.'[2] You have to go on. The past can inform us – we do well to take note and remember our heritage – but if we try to take refuge in it we shall end up ossified, theological dinosaurs who cannot serve our age. Faith that has no courage and dares not strike out in exploration, frightened to ask 'What if?', is not in the fullest sense faith. It is the childhood belief in Father Christmas that must be fostered by Mummy taking us to Lapland to prove that what we thought was true exists. We

---

2   Luke 9.62 RSV

don't need that kind of faith. The storms of life will take it down in the end. That kind of faith is shaken by watching our child die from cancer, by living through the loneliness of those we trusted forsaking and reviling us, by losing our jobs and our homes. The only faith that will stand the test is the sort rooted in reality; there is no substitute for making the journey ourselves.

Resist spoon-fed Christianity. Ask questions. Go and look. Go and see. Be courageous. If you find out it's not the way they always told you, well, be glad!

Come with me, then, and let's explore the living way of the Scriptures.

The Ancestors, the Book and the Way

As we think about the development of our faith practice, we must consider our sources of authority. Whom or what do we believe? Whom or what do we revere? To whom or what do we turn?

Living faith almost invariably has a community context. In the modern world, life as a reclusive solitary is made easier by the electronic revolution, hermits find it easier to make a living and the numbers of *hikikomori*[3] are rising – but even today, while spiritual faith remains intensely personal, it is characterized by group adherence. Thanks to the world wide web, it is now more possible than ever to belong to small and far-flung groups. For instance, the numbers of plain-dressing Conservative Quakers in the UK are very few, so their meetings are held online. Faith leads to sharing; faith groups normally stress the importance of adopting and upholding group belonging. This is certainly so in Christianity, where the faithful are

---

3 *Hikikomori* (Japanese) – reclusive teenagers and adults exhibiting extreme social withdrawal and confinement persisting for months and years. It is thought that on a conservative estimate 500,000 young Japanese people live as modern-day hermits (not in the religious sense, merely withdrawn from society). This phenomenon is reported in Europe, America, India and Asia, too.

described as the living stones built together to form the temple of God's presence, and the letter to the Hebrews says:

> Let us hold fast the confession of our hope without wavering, for he who promised is faithful; and let us consider how to stir up one another to love and good works, not neglecting to meet together, as is the habit of some, but encouraging one another, and all the more as you see the Day drawing near.[4]

In all human social groupings, hierarchies of authority develop. Even in co-operatives and egalitarian collectives, status hierarchies naturally form, and authority is accorded to individuals recognized and trusted by the group (like the formal status of Clerk in a Quaker Meeting, and the informal status of 'weighty Friends'[5]).

Sources of authority in faith groups don't need to be physically present – as in the Anglican Church where most members have never met the Archbishop of Canterbury and do not know any members of the General Synod – and, crucially, death tends more to cement than diminish authority, as the individual passes into legend.

So emerges the figure of the Ancestor. There are *ancestors* (people in your family who died long ago) and then there are *Ancestors* – the dead held in especial reverence whose influence and authority persists. Many world religions revere their Ancestors. For Native Americans, the soul of the land and the souls of the ancestors are bound up to form a sense of Ancestry. In Mexico the Day of the Dead includes making offerings to the ancestors, as did the nine-day Parentalia observance of ancient Rome. In both Taoism and Buddhism, the ancestors are venerated – Thai, Chinese and Vietnamese homes often feature an altar for the ancestors as well as the

---

4 Hebrews 10.23–25 RSVA

5 'Weighty Friends' – those within the Meeting who, by virtue of experience, long standing, good character and wisdom, are held in high regard.

usual devotional altar. It's important to understand this veneration is not worship – the Ancestors are not (necessarily) deities. The reverence is an expression of filial respect, and the relationship is one of continuing (abiding) influence.

The Ancestors stand in all the traditions of world religions. This is why the dilemma of children whose parents are divorcing is so acutely painful. It is not only about love and separation, the familiar breaking up before their eyes. It's also that we are religious beings, born to reverence. The child sees the Ancestors she has been taught to revere and obey turn against one another and betray one another, trading insults and going their separate ways. How can trust in what is held holy be rebuilt? How can so-called authority feel like firm ground again? The Ancestors are not far from the archetypes that determine our construction of spiritual understanding. Those we identify as our Ancestors will influence the maturation of our practice and belief, for Ancestor influence spreads beyond established and family lines. The great Vietnamese Buddhist teacher Thich Nhat Hanh, author of *Living Buddha, Living Christ*[6], studied the New Testament and the Christian faith, and while he continued to identify as Buddhist, he also acknowledged the powerful influence of Jesus upon his thought and practice. He expressed this by including a picture of Jesus among the others on his Ancestor shrine.

In the Nicene Creed, the Church is described as 'catholic and apostolic', and the Apostles' Creed declares belief in 'the communion of saints'. As well as expressing faith kinship beyond the boundaries of space and time (so, with other Christians in far off lands and members of the faith who have died), this imports the beginnings of an authority structure. Because the apostles were also the Apostles, and the saints developed into the Saints – canonization of

6 *Living Buddha, Living Christ*, Thich Nhat Hanh, first published by Rider Books in 1996, **ISBN-10:** 0712672818, **ISBN-13:** 978-0712672818

revered members of the Christian family, now deceased, intensified the reverence accorded to them. The Church is replete with Ancestors. The filial piety and reverence due to an Ancestor makes it very rude to challenge their wisdom and insight. In the 40 years of my membership of the Methodist Church, I have never heard any Methodist leader say John Wesley was wrong about anything. Wesley was an eccentric man, to say the least, and the Methodist Church strives (valiantly but not entirely successfully) for egalitarianism, but John and Charles Wesley have certainly achieved Ancestor status in that denomination.

The desert fathers, the church fathers, and the many long-dead canonized faithful – those who are not merely saints in the credal sense but made saints by official church decree – are regarded with such veneration that the authority of their influence is established. It becomes difficult to say they were wrong.

The Anglican Church upholds Richard Hooker's methodology of integrating scripture, reason and tradition in establishing Christian practice and belief. John Wesley later added personal experience, creating what the Methodist Church calls the Wesleyan Quadrilateral of sources of authority: scripture, reason, tradition and experience. In training its preachers, Methodism encourages individuals to consider how, for them personally, the weight or balance of authority falls.

It is often thought that in the Catholic and Anglo-Catholic wings of the Church, the emphasis is on the authority of the tradition; among charismatics, experience counts more heavily; while for Evangelicals, the weight falls upon the authority of Scripture. Yet these assumptions can significantly cloud underlying realities. For example, the Catholic rosary focuses meditation on events from the life of Mary that are for the most part derived from the Bible, thus creating reverence strongly rooted in Scripture. And among Evangelicals, the wisdom of Scripture is received through the lens of revered individuals – John Wycliffe, Martin Luther, George

Whitefield, Charles Spurgeon, Billy Graham, John Stott, David Watson, David Pawson and so on – and perhaps today Tom Wright is added to the list as a yet living Ancestor, thus establishing authority not by Scripture so much as by Evangelical tradition.

In the Scriptures themselves, Ancestors also emerge – the patriarchs and prophets of the Old Testament and the Apostles of the New. As the Christian faithful through the ages develop and establish an orthodoxy of practice, they look to the canonized saints and the canon of Scripture for their authority. They turn to the Ancestors and the Book.

But there's also the matter of Richard Hooker's 'reason' and John Wesley's addition of 'experience'. To the Ancestors and the Book we must add the Way – what members of the church family have found for themselves, whether by systematic scholarship and research or by a direct sense of the inner voice of the Spirit. For some, the weight of authority falls decisively on reason and/or experience. For example, George Fox at Pendle Hill:

> At night we came to an inn, and declared truth to the man of the house, and wrote a paper to the priests and professors, declaring the day of the Lord, and that Christ was come to teach people Himself, by His power and Spirit in their hearts, and to bring people off from all the world's ways and teachers, to His own free teaching, who had bought them, and was the Saviour of all them that believed in Him.[7]

Thomas Cranmer also upheld the direct personal headship of Christ over his Church, as distinct from that authority residing in ecclesiastical Ancestors (in that case, the Pope). At his last interrogation that led to his death by burning at the stake, Cranmer answered the questions of his examiner Thomas Martin:

7   From his Journal, 1651.

Martin: Now sir, as touching the last part of your oration, you denied that the pope's holiness was supreme head of the church of Christ.
Cranmer: I did so.
Martin: Who say you then is supreme head?
Cranmer: Christ.
Martin: But whom hath Christ left here in earth his vicar and head of his church?
Cranmer: Nobody.

This shifts the emphasis of authority from the Ancestor and the Book to the Way – direct personal communion with the risen Christ, shaped by the properly cautious addition of reason.

Now, the Way can mean the hallowed Way of Christian practice through the ages (the influence of our Christian history), or it can mean the unfolding of the sacred gospel of our lives (the continuing influence of the Spirit to which we bear witness).

You can see such decision-making under discussion in St Paul's letters to the Corinthian church about women wearing head coverings:

Does not nature[8] itself teach you that for a man to wear long hair is degrading to him, but if a woman has long hair, it is her pride? For her hair is given to her for a covering. If any one is disposed to be contentious, we recognize no other practice, nor do the churches of God.[9]

Here he is calling on three sources of authority: 'nature itself', 'we' (himself and others recognized by the Church as apostles), and 'the

---

8   The Greek (*physis*) means natural order. Paul doesn't mean that in nature a man's hair doesn't grow, but that by the way things/life/society naturally develop, we see men with short hair and women long.

9   1 Corinthians 11.14–16 RSV

churches of God' (the weight of consensus). The consensus in the Church and the testimony of natural order are part of the authority of the Way – the hallowed path. The authority represented by 'we' is that of the Ancestors (the heavyweights in the community). And for us reading today is added the authority of the Book: his precious fragments of letters have become part of the canon of holy Scripture.

So the Way may be the well-trodden path made holy by the footprints of the faithful throughout the ages. We look to the Way as an authority because we don't want to be isolated, because it is hard to go against the flow, because we seek acceptance and belonging. The Way is the orthodox expression of our tradition – and there are many orthodoxies; what is understood to be true in the Catholic tradition can be strongly contested by the Evangelical. So we look to the Way of our group, and we listen to its Ancestors, and to a great extent our religion is a chorus of tribal cries.

But so long as there is life, the story remains unfinished, and this is perhaps especially true in a religion with resurrection at its heart. New life emerges from even the sealed tomb. The Ancestors are those we revere from the past, but we also grow into our own calling and make our own souls – we may become the Ancestors of Christians yet unborn. We don't even need to be scholarly or gifted, only part of the communion of saints, our feet added to the thousands and thousands that tread and mark out the Way for others to follow. And thus the list of Ancestors is not yet closed, and the Way is still open; change and development are therefore still possible.

Likewise the Book, though the canon of Scripture is fixed, continues to unfold. The living word is still being written in our hearts and lives:

> I will put my law within them, and I will write it upon their hearts; and I will be their God, and they shall be my people. And no longer shall each man teach his neighbour and each

his brother, saying, 'Know the Lord,' for they shall all know me, from the least of them to the greatest, says the Lord.[10]

There is an unfolding landscape, a continuing creating and a continuing revelation of faith. Just as the written Scripture is by the witness of our experience a living book that works with power in our hearts, so the lived gospel of our day-to-day discipleship is sacred and has the power to transform: 'in my flesh I complete what is lacking in Christ's afflictions for the sake of his body, that is, the Church . . .'[11]

This is of course a matter of dispute in the Church. There are many who say the word of the Bible is the final authority on any matter (provided it is interpreted according to the Ancestral wisdom of their own tradition). There are those who will hear only wisdom that bears the mark of their Ancestors – the *imprimatur* of their own tradition. There are those for whom the Way is protected along its entire length by signs cautioning DO NOT WALK ON THE GRASS. For them, the Scripture, the Ancestors and the Way are already defined and determined, and the gospel they proclaim must bear the accreditation of consistency with the establishment; that's how we know what is and is not heresy.

But while the finished or unfinished nature of the gospel may be a matter of dispute on the *proclaiming* end, on the *receiving* end, it is beyond dispute unfinished. In the lives of Richard Dawkins and Ricky Gervais the revelation is not finished – the light hasn't even approached dawn. The revelation is yet to unfold, and the gospel has yet to be discovered. Perhaps this is true of us all. Perhaps the light we do not yet see already shines in our undiscovered Ancestors. Perhaps the truth we do not yet know still waits hidden in the Scriptures we have not understood. Perhaps the part of the narrow Way

10 Jeremiah 31: 33–4 RSV

11 Colossians 1.24 RSV

we have not yet walked holds some surprises in its vistas, in its twists and turns. Only time will tell. But surely the light is not shining full strength until it is received – it is made complete in us; the revelation is not accomplished until we have received it. And dare we ever say our understanding is complete even if the revelation is finished? Therefore, the search still unfolds, and the Way continues – there is always more to learn, whatever our tradition and personal conviction about the state of the revelation.

It is vital that we include in our understanding of faith this interior flowering in the soul. For instance, when the household of faith comes together in the celebration of the Eucharist – there is the chalice, and the wine is poured into it, and then there is the mystery of *epiclesis* or invocation when the Spirit unites with the elements. The wine is for drinking and the Spirit comes to transform us; let us never be those who settle for saying the words and checking the vintage and industriously polishing the silver.

Before we move on . . .

let's reflect

1 Who have your Ancestors been? Whose voices have conditioned your thinking, and whose example has shaped your life? Whom do you revere? Has this remained unchanged? Have you ever been disappointed in your Ancestors, discovering they were after all only idols with feet of clay? Have you ever had to stop and undertake an Ancestor review? Did you ever have to sack your Ancestors and start again? If you were to build a shrine for your Ancestors, whose pictures would you frame in gold or silver or simple wood, and install on your altar?

2 What is your relationship with the Book? How do you read it? Is it, for you, a collection of historical texts that helps us track our past, that you take into account as you shape your own

philosophy for yourself? Or do you read it as an almost magical book, each verse charged with potency – could you open it at random and let the first verse your eyes rest on be the headline of your day? How do you relate to the sacred text of the Bible? How has it shaped your life? And has this remained unchanged, or are there significant differences between how you used to read it and how you read it now?

3 What is the Way you are walking? Who are your companions on the journey? Do you rejoice in treading a Way paved with stones worn by many feet – holding precious the teaching and example of those who have gone before you? Or is the Way for you more like a difficult jungle track you approach with a machete in your hand? Is it a lonely struggle and are you a solitary explorer? How do you experience the Way?

4 Take four even rectangles of card or paper (such as the backs of four business cards, or four postcards or envelopes). Write four words on your rectangles (one word on each rectangle): SCRIPTURE, TRADITION, REASON, EXPERIENCE. Spend a little while moving them around in relation to each other, until you find the configuration that best represents the relationship in your life to these sources of authority in the formation of faith. In a line? In a stack? Three as a foundation and one on top?

5 Take a little time to turn these things over in your mind. Maybe go for a walk while you think them through.

And let's move on, now, to thinking about the relationship between men and women in the Church, and how the variance between their relative status has been shaped and conditioned by the Ancestors. Let's consider the story on this matter as it is offered us by our Book. And let's look not only at how the Way has developed in the past, but also toward our horizons, at the Way ahead.

2

Original blessing and original sin

Original sin

Matthew Fox's book *Original Blessing*[1] blew into the church with freshening force and power, challenging the establishment position hardened into place over centuries of consolidation.

Fox claimed to be offering a whole new direction for Christianity, grounded in the Jewish roots of Jesus. The foundation of what he called the 'Via Positiva' – the path of joy and gratitude, delight in creation – is the reconfiguration of our understanding of humanity as originally conditioned not by sin, but by blessing.

It may help to clarify what is meant by 'original' before going any further.

Christian theologians don't contest the view that humanity was originally blessed in the sense that Adam lived in a state of blessing before the Fall. His original condition *in the sense of his first state* was blessing – and that is and has always been accepted. So the doctrine of original sin is not denying there ever was a period of blessed innocence in the life of Adam, expressed in the opening chapters of Genesis by his location in the garden of Eden. Original sin doesn't simply mean the introduction of sin into the world at the Fall, after which all humans inherited a tendency to sin. It also means that the *tendency* to sin is already innate, offering the possibility, likelihood or inevitability of becoming manifest as a choice to sin (disobey God). It is the snake in the garden as well as the eating of the fruit. The questions

1   *Original Blessing: A Primer in Creation Spirituality* (1983), Bear & Company revised ed. 1996, ISBN 1-879181-27-4, *Original Blessing: A Primer in Creation Spirituality Presented in Four Paths, Twenty-Six Themes, and Two Questions*,(2000) Jeremy P. Tarcher/Putnam, ISBN 1-58542-067-0

challenging the minds of Christian theologians in the church's earliest days were the obvious ones: 'Where did it come from? How did it get there? What went wrong?'

The church fathers regarded Adam as a figure of history rather than as a representative figure in faith story. This is important in coming to understand some of the views that developed among them about both how sin entered the human race and how human sinfulness in general proceeds from Adam's sin in particular – and how it relates to Eve.

Going right back to Irenaeus in the second century, we find an emphasis on the creaturely nature of Adam – that his status as a creature implied an immense and profound separation between Adam and God, which made him an easy prey for Satan. This combined with his immaturity as a being – Irenaeus saw Adam as created with a naive and childlike mind intended by God to mature into spiritual wisdom – to create a dangerous weakness exploited by the opportunism of Satan.

Clement of Alexandria, Irenaeus's contemporary, likewise identifies immaturity as a strong component of the problem. He saw Adam as ignorant, unaware of God's purposes, and choosing to indulge in sexual intercourse before God's appointed time, and thus falling into sin.

Tertullian[2], born in the mid-second century, taught that the human soul is not pre-existent, is not created later, descending into the body after birth, but proceeds equally with the body from the parents – i.e. is incorporate with the developing unborn child. Tertullian saw every human soul as having its nature in Adam – being born as his descendant – and carrying that associated uncleanness until it is born again in Christ.

Inching forward to the late second century, we find Origen in the

---

2 Just as a matter of interest, Tertullian was the first Christian theologian to use the word *Trinitas* (Trinity) of God.

tradition of Platonism, arguing that every human soul is originally created by God and has the choice to advance towards or fall away from God – Christ alone choosing the former option. Unlike Tertullian, Origen believed in a pre-existent (pre-cosmic) human soul for whom sin became inevitable once in a physical body. Thus for Origen, the stain of sin was inherent in our physical state, regardless of what our personal choices might have been.

In the early-to-mid third century, Athanasius introduced a variation of perspective. He agreed with Origen that man's creatureliness made sin inevitable, but identified the source of blame not as the pre-existent soul but as proceeding from the inherent corruptibility of the clay from which God formed Adam. Adam fell because he took his eyes away from God and allowed the material aspect of his nature to distance him from the divine and cause him to sink into the corruption to which his flesh was heir.

In the second half of the third century, Gregory of Nyssa begins the move towards laying the blame on Eve. Though all the church fathers are quick to note the serpent's use of Eve as a vehicle of temptation, until this point the Fall was usually portrayed as an act of joint responsibility. Gregory had the thought that God foresaw Adam would sin and so planned the subdivision of humanity into male and female. Though he was not the first of the church fathers to link sin with sexuality, he led the move towards the view of Eve's responsibility for Adam's sin.

When we come to the Latin fathers of the fourth century, the theological tradition begins to adopt the familiar shape we recognize. Ambrose proposes that Adam's sin was essentially pride, and the anonymous Ambrosiaster adds the perspective that ambition (wanting to be as God) is the heart of the problem. He said that Adam's choice made the Devil God, thus placing Adam in Satan's power. This new idea, drawing upon the teaching of Jesus[3] that sin comes

---

3   Mark 7.15, Matthew 15.11

from within a man not from anything outside, moves the locus of responsibility from what is external to Adam, to his interior self.

It is this shift in thinking to an internalization of sin that lays the ground for Augustine's[4] teaching on original sin. Augustine was the main source of discussion on this matter in the Church and the main influence on its direction and development.

Despite the assertions of Pelagius that every soul possessed free will and could not be held accountable for sins committed by someone else, and that human sinfulness was not inevitable despite the ubiquitous habit of disobeying God, Augustine adopted the view that every child inherited the infection of sin. Because Adam was a creature, his mutable nature predisposed him to sin, and the entire human race became both corrupt and damned, condemned to sinning and giving birth to sinners. Augustine thought children caught the disease of sin from the lust excited in sexual intercourse and asserted that free will in the fullest sense was lost at the Fall because human nature is now tainted by evil.

By the fifth century Augustine's view held sway over that of Pelagius, and the Second Council of Orange in 529 adopted the Augustinian view of original sin, notwithstanding the objections of John Cassian and Vincent of Lérins.

The Council of Orange declared the whole man, both body and soul, to be changed for the worse through Adam's sin, but leaving the freedom of the soul unimpaired and only the body subject to corruption. Invoking Romans 5.12[5], Ezekiel 18.20[6] and 2 Peter 2.19[7], the Council concluded Adam's sin affected not himself alone but the whole human race, passing to his descendants also, and that sin is the death not only of the body but also of the soul.

---

4   Augustine of Hippo, not Augustine of Kent.

5   Romans 5.12 RSV – Therefore as sin came into the world through one man and death through sin, and so death spread to all men because all men sinned.

6   Ezekiel 18.20 RSV – The soul that sins shall die.

7   2 Peter 2.19 RSV – [W]hatever overcomes a man, to that he is enslaved.

These are the conclusions of our Christian Ancestors – we may not be aware of them, and once we are, we may disagree with what they thought. But they are our Ancestors and their power is only intensified by the distance clumping them into a complex blur of 'the past'. Those who are our pastors and teachers today have been trained in the thinking of our Ancestors – loyalty and orthodoxy are required as a discipline of the tradition.

Original blessing

Fast forward now to the closing decades of the twentieth century when, into the bleak and familiar landscape of the church tradition, erupts the colourful figure of Matthew Fox, Dominican priest. Influenced by Thomas Merton, exponent of Creation Spirituality, a cheerful and exotic figure with his yoga and his masseuse, his insistence on calling God 'Mother' and his refusal to condemn homosexuality, Fox earned the deep, deep suspicion of Cardinal Ratzinger, head of the Congregation for the Doctrine of the Faith. When the investigation Ratzinger required the Dominican Order to conduct found no heresy in Fox's writings, Ratzinger ordered another investigation, and in 1988 instructed Fox to stop teaching for a year for questioning the doctrine of original sin. Fox submitted, but resumed after the year expired, and in the early 90s was expelled from the Dominican order, received by the Anglicans as an Episcopal priest the following year.

Matthew Fox wanted to refocus our gaze away from original sin and onto original blessing. Again, it's important to be clear about what 'original' means. One should think in terms of endogenous and indigenous rather than merely 'first'; not just the manifestation of a first sin, but the roots of human propensity to sin. Fox doesn't merely mean Adam was innocent before he fell – all Christendom knows that. He means that a human being's natural state, our instinctive nature, what we bring to this world, the bent of our nature, tends towards goodness and love, towards a state of blessing, not towards a state of sin as Augustine thought. Fox believes we are born not infected but healthy, not damned but blessed.

He also averred that the doctrine of original sin was at variance with the Jewish faith and scriptures. Thinking through this brought into startling clarity for me the extent to which we see life through the lens of our Ancestors – that however we may protest that we are biblical Christians, people of the Book, we unwittingly read it with our understanding conditioned by the world view of our tradition, of our Ancestors.

When I came across Fox's assertion that Jewish faith knew nothing of original sin, my first thought was of Psalm 51, the *Miserere* sung in Lent to Allegri's painfully beautiful setting: 'Behold, I was shapen in wickedness: and in sin hath my mother conceived me'[8].

This is a psalm of King David, son of Jesse and anointed by the prophet Samuel. The famous nineteenth-century preacher and Bible scholar Matthew Henry says of this particular verse:

> David elsewhere speaks of the admirable structure of his body[9]; it was curiously wrought; and yet here he says it was shapen in iniquity, sin was twisted in with it; not as it came out of God's hands, but as it comes through our parents' loins. He elsewhere speaks of the piety of his mother, that she was God's handmaid, and he pleads his relation to her[10], and yet here he says she conceived him in sin; for though she was, by grace, a child of God, she was, by nature, a daughter of Eve, and not excepted from the common character.[11]

---

8   Psalms 51.5 Book of Common Prayer

9   He references Psalms 139.14–15

10 He references Psalms 116.16 and Psalms 86.16

11 Matthew Henry, *Commentary on the Whole Bible vol.iii Job to Song of Solomon*

Pick up almost any Christian commentary, and this is the perspective expressed – that the verse is a miniature exposition of the Christian doctrine of original sin. But it is not so.

If you explore Jewish commentary (there are several online), you will come across the story of King David's mother. David's father Jesse was the grandson of Boaz and Ruth, the Moabite. His wife (according to the Talmud, she is not named in the Bible) was Nitzevet, who had a Canaanite maidservant. Jesse, a righteous – even scrupulous – Jew, became obsessed by the legitimacy of his lineage. Boaz had died the night after he married Ruth, but she had conceived Obed, Jesse's father, in that brief union. After Boaz's death, however, the usual chorus of naysayers began to criticize Ruth, suggesting that because she was a Moabite, the marriage was illegitimate. This worried Jesse, and though he and Nitzevet were happily married with several sons, he resolved to part from her because their marriage was forbidden if his status as an Israelite was questionable while hers was authentic. So Jesse separated from her, but longed for a child of lineage undefiled by sin – and he came up with a plan: to have a child with the Canaanite maidservant. If his own Israelite status was authentic, as a Jewish convert she'd be free to marry him; if it were not, then she could still marry a Moabite as a Canaanite.

The maidservant listened politely to Jesse explaining this complex arrangement, then went to tell her good friend Nitzevet about it, proposing that on the wedding night they would swap places, as Leah did with Rachel in the case of Jacob[12]. This they did, and as a result of the union, David was conceived and born. Because Jesse had separated from Nitzevet, her pregnancy was assumed to be the result of union with someone else – so David was reviled by his (much older) brothers and regarded as the shameful offspring of adultery. That's how he came to be sent away to take care of the sheep and not invited

---

12 Genesis 29.21–30

to be in the line-up of brothers when God sent the prophet Samuel to anoint the new king from among the sons of Jesse.

As for being 'shapen in wickedness', the word 'shapen' (*chôlaletiy*) derives from the word *chûl*, which originally meant twist or whirl, but came to mean writhe in pain, particularly in connection with childbirth. So Psalm 51.5 is specifically about David's birth and conception – what it exactly does *not* mean is that he was inherently formed wicked in himself or by God.

It is at this point that I begin to wonder if it is even *possible* to sack one's Ancestors. The amount of exploration needed and the degree to which one's mind must remain open, in order to unpick the conditioning of one's tradition, is staggering – seemingly unending.

Matthew Fox is quite right. The Jewish position on sin is that a person has a choice. It is well summarized in the Bible in the book of Deuteronomy[13]:

> See, I have set before you this day life and good, death and evil. If you obey the commandments of the Lord your God which I command you this day, by loving the Lord your God, by walking in his ways, and by keeping his commandments and his statutes and his ordinances, then you shall live and multiply, and the Lord your God will bless you in the land which you are entering to take possession of it. But if your heart turns away, and you will not hear, but are drawn away to worship other gods and serve them, I declare to you this day, that you shall perish; you shall not live long in the land which you are going over the Jordan to enter and possess. I call heaven and earth to witness against you this day, that I have set before you life and death, blessing and curse; therefore choose life, that you and your descendants may live, loving the Lord your God, obeying his voice, and cleaving to him; for that means life to you and

---

13 Deuteronomy 30.15–20 RSV

length of days, that you may dwell in the land which the Lord swore to your fathers, to Abraham, to Isaac, and to Jacob, to give them.

'I set before you life and death, blessing and curse; therefore choose life' – is the position of Judaism on our relationship with God.

If we turn from the Ancestors to the Book, we find some very compelling evidence in favour of Matthew Fox's position. In the story[14] of the rainbow at the conclusion of the Great Flood, God establishes a covenant not only between God and Noah and Noah's sons, but also between God and every creature on earth. How could God, who is Spirit, enter a covenant relationship with what was purely material, physical? How could God, who is good, enter a covenant relationship with what was inherently infected with sin? That wouldn't make sense. There is an inherent implication and assumption that, however flawed may be humanity and the creation of which it is a part, at the core lies goodness, with which God has established a covenant.

Then, the descriptions of how life comes to be suggest that all life is spiritual, not merely material, and comes from God who is good. In particular, the use of the Hebrew word *nephesh* (living being) is strongly suggestive of the spiritual nature of all life.

In the second creation account of Genesis 2, we read[15]: 'The Lord God formed man of dust from the ground, and breathed into his nostrils the breath of life; and man became a living being.'

The name Adam is a play on the Hebrew word for earth (*adamah*); in effect, God has called him Earthling, because he is made from the dust of the earth. It could not be clearer that the materiality of Adam's being is without life until God breathes (the word used is for just a little puff) into his nostrils and Adam becomes a *nephesh*, a living being. In ancient Hebrew, the word *ruach* can equally be

---

14 Genesis 9.8–17

15 Genesis 2.7 RSV

translated as wind, breath or spirit, so we immediately see that the breath of God, or Spirit of God, is the source of human life, human breath. Adam becomes a *nephesh*, a living being, when God puffs his *ruach* into the lifeless clay. Not only Adam, but all creatures are described as *nepheshes* – and this implies breath, will, soul, life and personhood.

At the core of blessing is surely the presence of God, the Spirit of God, the breath of God – the *ruach*. The evidence for original blessing is very strong.

The corrective offered to our insight and understanding by the work of Matthew Fox is inspiring and reviving. Nonetheless, it must be conceded – the church fathers did have a point. St Paul (Jewish to the core and by background a Pharisee) put his finger on the problem. It might be a matter of simple choice ('therefore choose life'), but:

I do not understand my own actions. For I do not do what I want, but I do the very thing I hate. Now if I do what I do not want, I agree that the law is good. So then it is no longer I that do it, but sin which dwells within me. For I know that nothing good dwells within me, that is, in my flesh. I can will what is right, but I cannot do it. For I do not do the good I want, but the evil I do not want is what I do. Now if I do what I do not want, it is no longer I that do it, but sin which dwells within me.
So I find it to be a law that when I want to do right, evil lies close at hand. For I delight in the law of God, in my inmost self, but I see in my members another law at war with the law of my mind and making me captive to the law of sin which dwells in my members. Wretched man that I am! Who will deliver me from this body of death? Thanks be to God through Jesus Christ our Lord![16]

---

16 Romans 7.15–25 RSV

It is for exactly the reasons Paul expresses here that the church fathers spent so much time in study and discussion, trying to make sense of the paradox of human nature – on the one hand its nobility, integrity, beauty and goodness, on the other hand its baseness and cruelty, its decadence and sensuality. Evidently, the matter was not foreign to the Jewish mind.

In modern times (well, comparatively), it was that most Jewish of poets, Leonard Cohen, who summed up the enigma of the human condition in his song *Anthem* where he advises that we forget our aspirations to making any unblemished offering. He speaks of our flawed humanity in terms of a crack that runs through everything – but he offers the insight, so shrewd and full of hope, that it is precisely through this crack, the evidence of our brokenness and frailty, that light is able to enter our lives.

This is, it seems to me, an observation the church fathers would recognize and own, an understanding of the same grace they sought to express. In their teaching, they tied together baptism and original sin, the fall of Adam and our restoration in Christ, the second Adam. They insisted on the brokenness without exception of fallen humanity – but they, too, saw that this was where the light got in.

As W. H. Auden expressed it in his 1940 poem *Lullaby*, our humanity, even despite its mortality and its guilt, is entirely beautiful.[17]

Before we move on . . .

let's reflect

1 What do you personally believe about the natural original state of humanity? Sinful or blessed? Do you believe humans are born fatally flawed? Or are humans naturally kind and good, and the

---

17 The poem appears in Auden's collection, *Another Time*, published by Random House.

cruel and destructive elements later surfacing are to do with illness or social conditioning?

2 What do you believe about the Genesis creation story? Do you think Adam was in any sense a historical figure, or a mythological representation of humankind?

3 Thinking about the human race and society as a connected whole, to what extent do you think we are free to shape our own lives and thoughts, and to what extent are we so deeply conditioned that we unwittingly channel what we have been taught even when we mistakenly believe we are free? Can you identify moments in your life when you have tried (successfully or unsuccessfully) to break free from destructive habits of mind?

4 Athanasias believed the propensity to sin came not from Adam's soul, but from the clay out of which God made him. At first glimpse this idea seems laughably naive – but is it? To what extent do you think our bodies – for example our gut microbiome, our endocrine system, or our central nervous system – determine what appears to be our morality? For instance, children with ADHD are often characterized as 'naughty', and a brain tumour may be so located as to make a person aggressive (or conversely, passive). Mood often determines choices and may be linked to gut health. How far does the clay of which we are made influence our moral profile?

5 What do you think about the roles of blame and shame in managing human interaction? These have always been accepted and encouraged in the church as a means of controlling behaviour, but are increasingly seen as counterproductive and unhealthy. What methods would you choose for encouraging goodness and discouraging wrongdoing in human society?

And let's move on, now, to thinking about the creation of Adam and Eve, the relationship God created them to enjoy, the story of the Fall and the difference it made to their partnership.

3

The impact of the Fall

Some thoughts about reading the Bible

I trained for ordination on an Anglican course that also accepted Methodist students. This is not known as 'formation in ministry' for nothing. Ordination training is like being hammered on the anvil into previously unimaginable shapes. My friend who feared undergoing theological training lest he lose his faith was right to suspect that you don't come out the same as you went in.

On this course, an oft-repeated observation, faithfully handed down from each generation to the next, was that we threw everything we believed out of the window in the first year, and spent the next two years trying to figure out how to get it back in.

I had been brought up in rural Anglicanism, spent a decade as a Catholic, then wandered unintentionally into Methodism as a young mother in the early 1980s. In all those settings, the Bible was regarded with reverence as a source of authority, interpreted simply and assumed to be whatever it said it was. If it said Jesus was born of a virgin and rose from the dead, well, he was. If it said the letter to the Hebrews was written by St Paul, then it was. So we assumed. In the last two years of high school, Religious Studies at A-Level included an introductory tour of the different types of biblical criticism, but nothing that extended beyond a few paragraphs on notes copied from the blackboard into my exercise book.

And now, at ordination school, everything in the Bible came under the most rigorous scrutiny. Virtually nothing was written by who you always thought was the author, nothing was assumed to be true, and most stories of what people said and did were regarded as having been made up.

I thought about this very hard. What would be my source of authority now? The pathway I'd understood as a solid metalled road turned out to be more like walking on water, and how was I going to do that? I asked my tutors and my fellow students, but not only were they unable to provide an answer, they didn't even seem to see the problem because they'd never thought it was all true in the first place. But . . . I had.

I knew this book was more than just a collection of writings acquiring reverence through the status given it by august ecclesiastical bodies. I realized that much is lost in translation, that there were inherent contradictions in the text, that some of it was a patchwork of scraps and fragments. I knew the people of the ancient world saw things differently from us and sometimes communicated hidden truth through the symbolism of myth and archetype. And yet . . . I also knew the Bible to be a living book, capable of speaking to the condition of people lost and broken. I knew it shone with power, a book with a light inside.

The doctrinal standards[1] of the Methodist Church declare firmly:

The doctrines of the evangelical faith which Methodism has held from the beginning and still holds are based upon the divine revelation recorded in the Holy Scriptures. The Methodist Church acknowledges this revelation as the supreme rule of faith and practice.

And yet a 1998 Methodist Conference document on the Bible points out, 'When we talk about "the Bible" . . . we need to remember there is no definitive text . . . we cannot always be sure we know what was written in the "original" text.'

---

1 Found in *Constitutional Practice and Discipline of the Methodist Church Volume 2*, published by order of the Methodist Conference by Methodist Publishing, © (current year – revised annually) Trustees for Methodist Church Purposes.

The question I struggled with, as an ordinand, was how to retain my critical faculties in reading the biblical text while at the same time holding it as sacred. Where would I turn for my authority if *I had decided* (on the basis of study) what was true in the Bible? How would I know, then, what was true in me? No one could help.

And then I realized what our college principal[2] was doing when he preached an exegetical sermon and when he turned for divine inspiration to the Scriptures he dissected for a living. He had the art of *staying inside the text*, and I learned it from watching him and paying attention to what he did. A man of great humility, he taught us to ask 'What kind of God?' would be implied in our theology and practice and our reading of the Scriptures, and he showed us how to stay within the text and let it speak to us.

So as we come now to look carefully at the story of the Fall and its implications for the human race, I won't be setting myself above the text, discussing whether or not Adam and Eve were real human beings and snakes could speak in those days and the garden of Eden was a place. If you stay inside the text instead of setting yourself above it, you can simply explore what it is saying and understand it to the best of your ability. All human experience is replete with interpretation and seen through the mythological lens by which we understand the meaning of life. As a writer of fiction, I know the importance of accurate detail and characters who are true to life – because fiction is a carrier of truth just as history is often a vessel to safeguard nationalist mythology and even propaganda.

If we enter the story on its own terms, encountering it holistically, we can let it speak to us, exploring the landscape of its wisdom and allowing it to illumine our understanding.

We feel our way to a right reading of biblical story by looking for an alignment with our experience of life. This in turn means, of course, that our reading and interpretation of the Scriptures

---

2   The Ven. Martin Baddeley, 1936-2018

changes as we develop and mature. We don't lose the power of Scripture, but it deepens and enriches over time. To our reading of the Scriptures we bring our reason, experience and the traditions[3] of our faith, feeling down into the truth we trust is there waiting for us. The thing about spiritual truth is that it remains true whichever way you slice it – it is true in the home and the office and the farm and the marketplace and the prison and the refugee camp and the hospice, as well as in the college and the pulpit. Once you have that tough, effective, enduring, workaday faith, you have touched the bedrock of truth.

Equality in innocence

In English translation, the first three chapters of Genesis render the Hebrew references to God as either simply 'God' or as 'the Lord God' – so, either as a simple reference to the divine being, or with the amplification of dominant masculinity. This is fair enough as the English language perspective on divinity, but so much is lost in translation that it's worth our while to pause and consider.

Where the text in these three opening chapters of the Bible say 'God', it's a translation of the word *Elohim*. Where it says 'the Lord God', it's translating *Yahweh Elohim*.

Yahweh is given meaning in Exodus 3.14, where God (meeting Moses in the burning bush) declares his name to be I AM THAT I AM (or 'I will be what I will be'), but scholars caution us that this may be theological commentary incorporated into the Bible story on a name that has been emerging among the Hebrew people for some while. Some have suggested the name originated from *HWY* ('he blows'), in which we recognize immediate connections with the word *ruach* ('wind, spirit, breath'), and the *ruach* of God moving over the face of the deep as creation begins in Genesis 1. Others

---

3   Scripture, Tradition, Reason, Experience – Wesley's Quadrilateral.

have suggested the name comes from *HYH/HWH*, meaning 'cause to exist', abbreviating the phrase *ʾel ḏū yahwī ṣabaʾôt* – 'God who creates the hosts'.

El is the old Canaanite word for God, from which the Muslim *Allah* and the Jewish *Elohim* developed. The particularly interesting thing for us in this creation story about Adam and Eve, is that the word *Elohim* is a plural form that takes a singular verb. Where *Elohim* takes a plural verb, it then implies 'gods', but here in our creation story where it takes the singular verb, it is 'God'.

In Genesis 1, the story is told of the creation of humankind:

> Then God said, 'Let us make man in our image, after our likeness; and let them have dominion over the fish of the sea, and over the birds of the air, and over the cattle, and over all the earth, and over every creeping thing that creeps upon the earth.' So God created man in his own image, in the image of God he created him; male and female he created them.[4]

The use of 'us' in the text is not like the royal 'we' or the formal 'we' used in essay-writing, it's because *Elohim* is plural. This is the first germ of what over time becomes our doctrine of the Trinity, three persons in one God – creator, redeemer, sustainer – acting in harmony and unity with one purpose; the plural deity that takes a singular verb.

Elohim creates humankind in the divine image, and this implies the incorporation of diversity within unity – not a ranked hierarchy, first man then woman, but a co-equal unity of the image of God expressed in woman as also in man. In our English translation, it sounds as if the man (Adam not Eve) is created in God's image ('God created man in his own image, in the image of God he created him') with the female of the species as something of an afterthought

---

4 Genesis 1.26–27 RSV

('male and female he created them'), but the Hebrew says 'them' not 'him', making it clear that male and female together are made '*in our image*', in the image of this plural deity who takes a singular verb – diverse but unified.

At this point – though this is not our main focus so I won't dwell on it – it's worth pausing to note that our preachers and teachers interested in moral theology have made a great deal of the binary character of humanity – *male and female he created them* – and used it to denigrate or exclude people whose sexuality and gender differ from heterosexual cisgendered norms. However, both sexuality and gender come in very diverse forms, including hermaphrodite as well as homosexual, bisexual, heterosexual and transgender. It is entirely possible without forcing the text to see this creation story as understanding the whole diversity of male and female in all its expressions and combinations as incorporated into one diversity-within-unity image of God, none of it aberrant or creationally inauthentic. People are as they are, and Elohim made them so, and blessed them.

Moving on to the second creation account, in Genesis 2 we find Adam placed by God in the garden of Eden to till it and care for it, and instructed not to eat of the tree of the knowledge of good and evil, for 'in the day that you eat thereof, you will surely die' (v.17).

Then comes the creation of Eve, after God sees Adam is lonely. God makes all the animals and brings them to Adam, who forms a connection with them by naming them, but none of them is quite right for what is needed (though they do say a man's best friend is his dog, so that must have been a near miss). Then God puts Adam into a deep sleep, takes out one of his ribs, closes up the wound and makes Eve out of the rib.

God brings her to Adam, who says:

> This at last is bone of my bones
> and flesh of my flesh;

> she shall be called Woman,
> because she was taken out of Man.[5]

Matthew Henry, in his *Exposition of the Old and New Testament*, famously said:

> Women were created from the rib of man to be beside him, not from his head to top him, nor from his feet to be trampled by him, but from under his arm to be protected by him, near to his heart to be loved by him.

She is just called 'the woman' until right after the Fall (Genesis 3.20), at which point we learn that Adam has called her Eve because she is the mother of everyone living – 'Eve' (*Chava*) means 'Life'. So the two of them together, Earth and Life, made into *nephesh*es by the breath of God, are the wellspring of humanity.

Let's look closely at the role God intended for Eve. The term 'help-meet' emerged for what God intended. This derives from the earlier English forms of the biblical text, which translated the Hebrew description of God creating a helper suitable for Adam as: 'an helpe meet for him' (Genesis 2.18). 'Meet' used to mean proper or appropriate; for instance, in the *Sursum Corda* of the old *Book of Common Prayer Holy Communion*, the priest says, 'Let us give thanks to the Lord our God,' and the people reply, 'It is meet and right so to do.' When things meet, they are connected, they match, they are in their proper place. This is what is meant by Eve being a help 'meet' for Adam: one who is just right for him and for the role. The word 'mate' comes from 'meet'. The Hebrew word used, *kenegdo*, means 'corresponding to', or 'equal to'.

The 'help' part of 'helpmeet' has connotations of succour or rescue – she is coming to his aid. This is not the same as a 'home help' or

---

a 'handmaiden', someone who is there to do someone's bidding and take care of the chores. This same word 'help' in the Hebrew (*ezer*) and in the English is there, for example, in Deuteronomy 33.26, that speaks of God in majesty riding on the heavens to help you, or Psalm 33.20, '[The Lord] is our help and shield.' We also see it in the name of Moses' son Eliezer, which means 'God is my help', surely not intended to mean 'God is handy for minor secretarial roles and housework'.

Perhaps the most familiar and memorable instance of this word is its use in Psalm 121:

I will lift up my eyes unto the hills – from whence comes my help?
My help comes from the Lord, who made heaven and earth.[6]

If we move on from the Hebrew text to the Greek text of the Septuagint (the oldest Greek version of the Old Testament), we find the word for 'help' given here is *boēthos*, which can mean help either in the sense of assistance or of running to our rescue. The word for suitable or 'meet' here, is the Greek *kata*, which can mean 'according to' or 'by way of'. So the reading could be either that God created Eve by way of an assistant to Adam, or that God created Eve to come to Adam's aid as an equal or corresponding partner. The word *boēthos* originally derives from fusing two words meaning 'cry out' and 'run', and the verb *boētheō* means 'come to the rescue' or 'supply aid in cases of urgent need'. This word is used in the New Testament where the help of God or Jesus is needed[7].

When we look at the Hebrew together with the Greek, we find nothing at all to suggest that Eve was created for a role of subservience. The meaning is clear that God is creating someone fit to come

---

6 My paraphrase of the KJV Psalms 121.1–2, adding the vital question mark that makes all the difference. The Psalmist is saying, does my help come from the High Places (shrines of the Canaanite gods)? No, but from the Lord who made heaven and earth.

7 Matthew 15.25, Mark 9.22–24, Acts 16.9, 2 Corinthians 6.2, etc.

to Adam's rescue in his solitude, standing alongside him and working with him, contributing equally and made in God's image as Adam is.

In establishing biblical Christianity from the text, we would have to conclude that equality between men and women is their creation (i.e. pre-Fall) status. Nothing else is credible.

The story of the Fall

The story of the Fall is very familiar to us. In the garden where Adam and Eve live, there is a serpent, more crafty/subtle/cunning than any other creature God has made. You should not buy a used car from this snake.

This description of the snake as crafty flags up for us that its motive is suspect. We are interested in its approach, which is not to confront or argue with the boundaries laid down by God, but to question them: 'Did God indeed say you mustn't eat from any tree in the garden?'

A well-known principle of marketing is to prime the customer with a series of questions to which the answer will be 'Yes'. This creates a psychological barrier to changing track later, when the opportunity to purchase merchandise is offered; it becomes harder for the punter to say 'No'. Evidently the snake understood this clearly; it starts Eve questioning the will of God by encouraging her into a line of thought implying that God has been unreasonable in telling her not to eat from any and every tree – which he didn't. Eve has grasped exactly what God said, though, and responds earnestly that this isn't right. She explains that God did in fact say they could help themselves to the fruit, but not this particular tree, lest they die. The snake counters this with a flat contradiction – 'You won't die' – and suggests that God has a hidden agenda, that if she and Adam eat of the tree they will become like God, their eyes opened to discern between good and evil.

Evidently in giving houseroom to the idea, the process is already begun, for Eve sees that the fruit of the tree is good to eat. Her aspirations to be like God and tell what's good from what isn't have started. She decides the fruit *is* good to eat regardless of what God says and offers some to Adam, who eats it with her. And the snake's work is done. Adam sees everything differently. Next time God comes looking for him ('Where are you?'), Adam hides because he is ashamed of his nakedness, and God asks him, 'Who told you that you were naked?'

Themes emerging from the story of the Fall

Discriminating between good and evil

Why the ability to discern between good and evil is undesirable might not be immediately obvious to us. God told Adam and Eve not to eat of the tree because it would bring about their death. The snake told them they wouldn't die, but their eyes would be opened to discern the difference between good and evil. As soon as she listened to the snake (so the power of something begins when you start to pay attention to it), the woman 'saw the fruit was good to eat' – she began to make the distinction. And when they ate the fruit, just as the snake said, 'the eyes of both were opened, and they knew that they were naked; and they sewed fig leaves together and made themselves aprons'[8]; something that had been a neutral feature with no awkwardness attached to it now became a problem – a bad thing – in their estimation.

The culture of modesty has grown into something massive, and also become a significant issue of control of women by men. It all starts here, in how we perceive things, in a loss of innocence. If

---

8   Genesis 3.7

you stop and think about the experience of human life, you start to see that the inability to accept the way things are without angst and discontentment affects us adversely. Putting value judgements on everything is an absolute curse. Isaiah[9] challenged the problem inherent in separation when he said, 'I make weal and create woe, I am the Lord …'[10] The story of the Fall pinpoints the tragedy of the human inability to accept with serenity what the hand of God offers us, working with him in trust to bring the best out of our circumstances.

It is in fact curiously difficult to know what's good and what's evil. There's a wonderful old story in the Taoist tradition addressing this:

An old farmer had worked the land to raise crops for many years. One day his work horse ran away. When they heard the news, his neighbours came to commiserate. 'What bad luck,' they sympathized. 'Maybe yes, maybe no,' the old farmer said.

The next morning the horse returned, bringing three wild horses along with it. 'How wonderful,' the neighbours exclaimed in delight. 'Maybe yes, maybe no,' the old man said.

The following day, his son tried to begin riding one of the new horses, was thrown from it and broke his leg. The neighbours shook their heads and pronounced this new development to be a serious misfortune. 'Maybe yes, maybe no,' said the farmer.

The very next day, army officers came to the village to conscript all the young men to fight in the war. Because the son's leg was broken, they left him behind. The neighbours, whose own sons had been taken away to risk their lives in battle, congratulated the farmer on his good luck. 'Maybe yes, maybe no,' he replied.

---

9   Chapter 45, his address to Cyrus, see 'What is the snake?' section, below.

10   Isaiah 45.7 RSV

The ability to accept one's circumstances and trust God from whose hand all things come, brings peace. Adam and Eve chose a different road, and it brought them heartache.

What does this mean, then about making value judgements? Are we supposed to simply embrace everything that comes our way as equally acceptable, however opportunistic, abusive or predatory it may be? I don't think that's the intention of the story of the Fall – the message is that, since no one can know everything, we must exercise caution in choosing whose recommendations we will follow, to whose voice we will listen. And we will hearken to our Ancestors and our tradition in applying our reason and experience to discern the way of God.

This is about the difference between discernment and discrimination – Eve thought, when the snake said she would be able to tell good from evil, that she would be getting discernment. What she actually got, inadvertently chose, was discrimination; and this is the heart of the curse upon her.

Taking the long view

In the Genesis story, Eve tells the snake God has warned them that if they eat the fruit of the tree they will surely die. The snake assures her this is not so; they will acquire the ability to discern good from evil like God. Eve and Adam do eat the fruit, and it turns out like the snake said – the power of discrimination and making value judgements begins. So – was God wrong?

This is surely about taking the long view. Adam and Eve did not die on the day they ate of the fruit, but death came into the world on that day as a result of it, according to the story.

This reminds me of a time I sat at a bus stop waiting for the 305 to come by and take me home. It was the end of the school day, and nearby in a shop doorway stood a group of young teenage boys sharing the illicit pleasure of a cigarette. On the seat in the bus shelter, a small boy sat with his mother, watching the older children with horrified fascination. Eventually he asked her, 'Will they die if they smoke that cigarette?' She answered in loud tones ringing with moral disapproval, 'Yes! They will!' He watched them narrowly, but they didn't die. Some things take a long time to unfold – and even when they do, we don't always understand them. During the time I worked as a free-church chaplain in a hospice, a thin, exhausted man dying of lung cancer came in for rest and care. I sat at his bedside one day as he mused on the years that had gone by, and on his illness. 'They say smoking causes lung cancer,' he said, 'but it doesn't. I've smoked all my life.'

In the Genesis story of the Fall, we can see an emerging theme of the ability to make connections, to see that actions have consequences, and to take the long view.

Secrets and transparency

A thread about honesty and transparency as essential to healthy relationship runs through the story of the Fall. The snake hints to Eve that God has a hidden agenda and is concealing from her that his ability of discernment is hidden in the fruit. 'Maybe yes, maybe no,' as the old farmer said. She discovers that, yes, the ability to make value judgements is accessible to her by eating the fruit, but still the mystery of weal and woe is held in the hand of God. The work of the snake is to sow suspicion and distrust in the human mind.

When God comes looking for them in the garden, they are hiding from him. His call to Adam – 'Where are you?' – is surely one of the most heartbreaking moments in the Bible. In a culture of secrets and suspicion and hidden agendas, no real connection or true friendship is possible. Games of hide-and-seek are only fun when the person you are seeking really wants to be found. If night falls and supper time and bedtime pass by, and you are still crouched in the gap behind the wood shed, it just gets miserable and lonely and cold.

Openness, transparency, honesty and authenticity are essential to good health in our dealings with one another, and this is a theme that emerges in the story of the Fall.

Shame

Strongly linked in the story to both the appearance of value judgments and the beginning of secrets is the emergence of shame. Adam and Eve hide from God because they are naked, and they create clothing to hide their nakedness from view; they are ashamed. This brings into focus that nakedness is a concept, not a thing. It is the shame that creates the nakedness, not the other way round. Shame is one of the most destructive forces in human society, corrosive and crippling to the human soul, and that's why it belongs right here in the story of the Fall.

Listening

A clear theme in the story is a challenge about who claims our attention. Whom will we believe? To whom will we listen? Eve listens to God, takes in what he says and remembers it – but then she listens to the snake, and Adam listens to Eve. When God comes looking for them, he also listens to what they have to say for themselves. 'Because you have listened to the voice of your wife . . .' is the beginning of the curse of Adam.

Listening is a kind of hospitality, inviting a point of view into our minds. The story of the Fall asks us, to whom will you listen?

Accountability and blame

There's a theme about responsibility emerging in the story of the Fall, and it takes two forms: one healthy and one destructive.

The healthy form of responsibility is Adam and Eve's accountability to God. He has told them not to eat from the tree, and they are accountable to him. This theme of authority and accountability runs right through the Scriptures. The figures of the prophet and the king and the lawmaker are vested with authority, but it derives from the stream of authority flowing down from God. Woe betide the false prophet or the king who departs from God's command.

In the New Testament story of the centurion who comes to Jesus begging him to heal his *pais*, his young slave (with connotations also of being his sexual partner), Jesus says he will come home with him and heal the man. But the army officer replies:

> Lord, I am not worthy to have you come under my roof; but only say the word, and my servant will be healed. For I am a man under authority, with soldiers under me; and I say to one, 'Go,' and he goes, and to another, 'Come,' and he comes, and to my slave, 'Do this,' and he does it.[11]

What's interesting is that he recognizes that his power lies in being *under* authority – the power vested in him proceeds from something greater than himself; this is the principle of accountability, healthy responsibility.

A stark contrast is blame, that miserable parody of accountability, so prevalent in human society. Like shame, blame corrodes and cripples the spirit. One of the names for the devil in the Bible is 'the accuser of the brethren'[12]. By contrast, the Holy Spirit convicts, allowing us to see where we have become entangled in destructive words or actions (our own or those of others) and liberating us from their hold, but does not accuse us or crush us with blame.

In the story of the Fall, the snake puts a spin on God's motives that amounts to misrepresentation, unjustly blaming God for a disadvantage that is in truth no disadvantage. Adam blames Eve and Eve blames the snake and so begins the age-old tradition of passing the buck.

This theme develops further in Genesis 4, in the story of Adam

---

11 Matthew 5.8–9 RSV

12 Revelation 12:10 KJV

and Eve's son Cain murdering his brother Abel. God asks him, 'Where is your brother?' He replies, 'Am I my brother's keeper?' This refusal to take responsibility for one's own actions – refusal to be accountable – proceeds from, is the child of, the culture of blame.

The story of the Fall proposes to us that accountability brings about health in human relationships, but blame brings division and enmity.

What is the snake?

In reading the story of the Fall, we should be cautious in making assumptions concerning the serpent in the garden.

Standard Christian (not Jewish) commentary assumes this to be Satan and makes a link with the Book of Revelation[13] which speaks of a great dragon being thrown down, an ancient serpent identified as Satan and the devil.

We should bear in mind, though, that the incorporation into Judaism of Satan as a figure was patchy and owes much to Zoroastrian influence.

Zoroaster emerged in Persia (Iran) in a similar time frame to the emergence of Abraham in Iraq, and Zoroastrianism developed into an immensely influential cultural force in the ancient world. To understand something of the religious dialogue between Abraham's world view and Zoroaster's, it is helpful to read Deutero-Isaiah's prophecies addressed to Cyrus of Persia (in Isaiah 45).

Israel has much cause for gratitude towards Cyrus because he not only decreed the temple should be rebuilt but also provided the resources to enable this. The prophecy addressed to Cyrus is as positive and complimentary as one might expect. Yet, though couched in the most courteous and approbatory terms of approach, the

---

13 Revelation 12.9 and 20.2.

prophecy offers a strong and uncompromising challenge to the religious conceptual perspective of the Zoroastrian Cyrus.

'I form light, and I create darkness,' says the Lord to Cyrus in verse 7; 'I create wellbeing *and* I create woe. I, the Lord do *all* these things.' This counters the dualistic belief structure of Zoroastrianism, in which two deities – Ahura Mazda, god of light, health, cleanliness, wellbeing and order, and Angra Mainyu, god of darkness, disease, dirt, suffering and chaos – are locked in battle for the future of the world. Every choice of every human being strikes a blow for either Ahura Mazda or Angra Mainyu, and the invisible realm is also filled with spiritual hosts arraigned against one another, demons and angels fighting on either side.

From the world view of Abraham comes the central tenet of Judaism: 'Hear O Israel, the Lord your God, the Lord *is One*,'[14] in direct contradiction to Zoroastrian religious concepts. For Zoroastrianism, it is Angra Mainyu who is the god of darkness and disorder, and if Ahura Mazda defeats Angra Mainyu in battle, the world will be restored to the perfectly round shape it held at creation, the battle and the influence of Angra Mainyu having caused the lumps and dents of the mountains and valleys. Yet Isaiah throws down the gauntlet, saying: '*I* will go before you and level the mountains . . . and *I* will give you the treasures of darkness . . . I am the Lord, and there is no other.'

Deutero-Isaiah was probably writing in the sixth century BCE, and the various strands making up the Pentateuch (Genesis, Exodus, Leviticus, Numbers and Deuteronomy) consolidated around the fifth century BCE. These early writings, and the traditions on which they depend, are not late enough for the cultural influence of Zoroastrian dualism to have infiltrated the world view of the story. Though the book of Job mentions the satan, it's not a proper noun – not Satan – but any kind of accusatory or adversarial figure. The dualism of God

14 Deuteronomy 6.4.

versus Satan and the ranged armies of angels and demons on opposing sides do not emerge until the first or second centuries BCE and
do not develop significantly until the inter-testamental period; they
are not incorporated into the thinking of these early Jewish texts.

So, who is the snake in the garden of Eden, then? In Jewish
thought, the snake in this context usually represents evil (human)
inclination. Maimonides[15] associates the snake with the appetitive
faculty, by which he means the faculty that causes us to desire or to
loathe something, to pursue it or flee from it.

If we take the myth of the Fall to be the *story* of the human
condition, rather than the *origin* of the human condition, the presence of the snake makes more sense. It then becomes a warning
against capitulating to the voracity of our appetites that can play us
false and lead us out of the way of God's wisdom by appealing to
our cravings and proclivities. It lifts the story out of its confinement
within the linear progression of human moral development, into the
larger dimension of general application – for 'Adam and Eve', read
'you and me'.

God's curse laid upon the snake is that it would be cursed above
all wild animals and cattle, that it would be condemned to travel
about upon its belly and eat dust 'all the days of your life', and that
there should be enmity between the snake and the woman, between
all the woman's descendants and all the snake's descendants – '[her
seed] shall bruise your head, and you shall bruise his heel.'[16]

An interesting feature of this – the way God speaks to the snake –
is that it doesn't sound like a Satan-figure God is addressing. It is
definitely an animal, not a supernatural being, and retains its place
in the animal order. In terms of myth, it has more of a flavour about
it of: 'And that, boys and girls, is how snakes came to be so loathed
and so feared and so dangerous.'

---

15 Medieval Jewish philosopher, with weighty status as a rabbinic scholar.

16 Genesis 3.14-15 RSV

The curse of Adam

To Adam, God said:

> Because you have listened to the voice of
>   your wife,
>   and have eaten of the tree
> of which I commanded you,
>   'You shall not eat of it,'
> cursed is the ground because of you;
>   in toil you shall eat of it all the days of
>   your life;
> thorns and thistles it shall bring forth
>   to you;
>   and you shall eat the plants of the field.
> In the sweat of your face
>   you shall eat bread
> till you return to the ground,
>   for out of it you were taken;
> you are dust,
>   and to dust you shall return.[17]

The curse of Adam is not the focus of this book – we're thinking about the curse of Eve – but there is enough in here for another whole book of its own. The difficult relationship between Adam and the earth from which he is made, and after which he is named, is the focus of this curse. He was lifted up out of earth into life, but it will claim him again because of the choice he made. Assuming Adam to stand for humanity, there are so many implications here – about industrial struggle and human inequality and the resulting wars in the aggression of consumerism, about the human view of the earth as a frontier

---

17 Genesis 3.17–19 RSV

to be crossed and a conquest to be made, about climate change and our unwise relationship with the rhythms and systems and life forms of earth. Adam has raped the earth, and it is dying because of its relationship with Adam. He's not the only one returning to dust.

According to this curse of Adam by God, the root of the problem is 'Because you have listened to the voice of your wife...' As the saying goes, 'What you pay attention to, you get more of.' How life develops starts with where you place your attention, and the heart of the story of the Fall is its teaching about the crucial importance of fearing God – heeding God's commands unwaveringly.

The curse of Eve

But let's look in some detail at God's curse laid upon Eve in the Genesis story.

> To the woman he said:
> 'I will greatly multiply your pain in
>   childbearing;
>   in pain you shall bring forth children,
> yet your desire shall be for your husband,
>   and he shall rule over you.'[18]

In particular, let's focus on the significance of the word 'desire'. What is intended? The little words 'yet' and 'and' have influenced the different conclusions reached.

Some have linked the pain in childbirth with the desire and separated the husband's rule, coming to the conclusion that the first part of the curse is that despite the increased pain of childbirth, woman

18 Genesis 3.16 RSV

will still have the urge for sexual union, and thus be condemned – by her own irresistible desire – to bring pain upon herself.

Others have separated the composition of the curse differently, seeing the pain of childbirth as the first half, but linking the desire not with the childbirth but with the husband's rule. Under this reading, there is an implicit understanding of frustration, a mismatch, between what woman yearns for and what she actually gets. Her desire is for her husband, she has a longing for the beautifully matched union she once had, but what she gets is domination, subjugation. She looks for partnership and finds domestic enslavement.

Others have read it to mean that woman's own will must now be submitted to her husband's, that what she chooses will henceforth be under his governance. I find this interpretation interesting in that it certainly provides a religious justification for the domination of women by men, but I think it is not persuasive as an interpretative translation.

Still others, perhaps incorporating the earlier part of the story where it is Eve who influences Adam to eat the fruit, have understood this verse to mean that woman shall have the urge to dominate/possess/rule over her husband, but the tables will now be turned and he will rule over her. I find this interpretation to be somewhat fancifully drawn out of the text, so will set it aside. There is not sufficient implication of it in the Hebrew wording to warrant adopting this reading.

It's important to look carefully at the Hebrew word used for 'desire' and to bear in mind that wordplay is often used to deepen meaning in the Hebrew testament of the Bible[19]. The Hebrew word

---

19 A good example is the vision of summer fruits in Amos 8. The Lord asks Amos what he sees. The prophet says he sees a basket of summer fruit. The Hebrew word is *qayits*, used for fruit (mostly figs) gathered at the end of the summer, the end of the agricultural year. The Lord then replies: 'The end has come upon my people Israel. I will never again pass by them.' (Amos 8.1–2) The word for 'end' is *qēts*. Though the meanings are different, the wordplay joins them together, and textures the vision with the sense of something ripe and over-ripe, something for which the time has come and is even overdue. The prophetic message is that the end is coming for the northern kingdom.

in this case is *teshuqah*. It means yearning or longing for, originally 'stretching out after'. In the Greek Old Testament (the Septuagint), *teshuqah* is translated as *apostrophē*, which means a turning away from. Among the different shades of meaning associated with this word is that of turning away from other people towards one particular individual. In our verse (Genesis 3.16), the preposition used (*pros*, meaning towards) gives us a reading of woman turning away from others and towards her husband. This fits well with the Hebrew *teshuqah* (desire, longing, yearning), to give us a picture of woman longing for a special individual relationship of connection with her husband, but finding instead a role of servitude. She is looking for equality but finding domination, and this is the curse laid upon her.

There's further illumination in asking ourselves, from whom is Eve turning away? When she stretches after Adam, on whom does she turn her back? The meaning could be that woman turns from other potential partners or other human relationships towards an exclusive relationship with her husband. In modern English we sometimes refer to our sexual partnership as our 'primary relationship'. It could mean that. Or, the root of the curse could lie in Eve turning away from *God* in favour of Adam. This makes sense of the part about adoption of the husband's rule. If God is the one who should rule over us, whose will and wisdom should guide our lives, then turning away from his reign towards human will and guidance will bring trouble and sorrow. This reading brings out the justice inherent in the curse: 'You chose it; right, then, you've got it. You preferred human judgement over divine ordinance – right, then, you have it. Here it is. You turned away from God to Adam? Good luck.'

The created order is men and women living and working together in peace under the rule of God's guidance, God's authority. When Eve turns away from God towards Adam, it is inevitable that not only is the relationship between humanity and God disrupted, but so is the interrelationship between human beings. The creation order goes awry. There is still a hierarchy in place, but a broken one, not operating as intended. This balances with the curse laid on Adam, 'Because you listened to the voice of your wife...'; the nub of the matter is the turning away from God as the voice of authority to each other.

In cursing, as in blessing, there must always be inherent justice. A curse, like a blessing, has to find something it will stick to[20]. You cannot arbitrarily curse a person who doesn't deserve it – the curse won't stick. That's why some courses of action are inherently cursed or blessed; because, of themselves, they flow against or with the current of grace. This is not God throwing a hissy fit, wishing something nasty as a punishment upon Eve. God is the one from whom the structures of reality proceed. God is the creator of all that is. His strictures are not randomly despotic; they are inevitable components of reality. If Eve turns away from what God lays down towards conspiring alternatives with Adam, then *Adam is what she will get*. When God pronounces the curse, then, he is not like a judge giving sentence so much as the voice of reality explaining the consequences of what she herself chose. There are no alternatives. This is the result of her choice.

This justice and the balanced relationship between Adam and Eve could be the root of the pain in childbirth that forms the first part of the curse: 'I will greatly multiply your pain in childbearing.'

The word used for 'pain' here is *itstsâbôn*, meaning labour, hardship, sorrow or toil as well as pain. The 'childbearing' incorporates both conception and giving birth in the Hebrew text. As we have seen, the curse laid on Eve balances the curse laid on Adam to do with the struggle of bringing forth fruit from the land. So a picture emerges of a balanced, equal curse, with the addition of an unbalancing of the relationship to become domination instead of harmonious equality.

The conclusion we can reach is that the dominance of woman by

---

20 Ephesians 4.27, and John 14.30 rely on this understanding that evil requires a foothold.

man is not part of the natural order but part of the fallen order. It is a situation not to be accepted but to be redeemed. It is an indication of where things have gone wrong, not an inherent biological inevitability.

Before we move on . . .

let's reflect.

1 What is the snake? If we look at the story of the Fall not as an event in history but as insight into humanity, then the snake is there in the garden for everyone – for you and me. What is it? Do you see it as an external agent of temptation, or as a person's particular weakness . . . or . . .?

2 Some people of faith believe strongly in modest dress and conduct; others regard it as less important or even as repressive. The Genesis story offers the concept of nakedness as a state of mind rather than a condition in itself. What do you personally feel about modesty and nakedness?

3 Keeping secrets has traditionally been highly prized in the faith community – confidentiality, not gossiping, the secrets of the confessional, are all regarded as very important. Yet it's certainly the case that predatory and abusive individuals make use of this tradition of secrecy and discretion to divide and conquer and to prey on vulnerable people, binding them to secrecy. When Adam hid from God, their relationship was broken. What is the place of secrets?

4 How easy do you find it to distinguish good from evil? What are our safeguards and reference points in discerning? Whom do you trust?

5 Is there, in your view, a clear binary divide, such that women are more suitable for some roles in life than men? Are there some things women can always do better than men, and vice versa? Or

do these differences proceed from nurturing in cultural tradition? Are the real differences and suitabilities purely individual? What are your thoughts about gender roles?

And let's move on, now, to thinking about the legacy of the Fall on the faith community. How has this story influenced and shaped belief and practice in the church?

4

The legacy of the Fall

Nature and nurture

I watch the foxes in our garden, coming at dusk for the food I've put out for them. The dog fox is the big one claiming precedence in enjoying their meal. The vixen is the one rolling coquettishly on the ground beside the dish, snatching a mouthful when she thinks she can get away with it.

I watch the pigeons in the park. The cock bird is the one with his chest puffed out in grandiose display, persistently pursuing the hen bird, who is trying to go about her business searching for crumbs dropped by picnickers yet is not exactly rebuffing his advances.

I think of the deer on the hillsides, the stags fighting and bellowing, competing for the right to be the one who copulates with as many of the hinds as possible, the lord of the herd.

I think of the advice of vets and breeders, that if you want a sociable, playful cat or dog, choose a male – they are simpler and friendlier. Bitches and queens are more complicated and uncertain of mood, more solitary.

There is no doubt at all that the male of the species is different from the female. In human society, all around the world and in all religions, women are abused and made to take a lower place, widows are often degraded and blamed for the death of their husbands, rape is a weapon of war and women are commodified for sex and domestic service. It is clear that this arises from the norms of our species manifesting in general, not from the Christian religion in particular. Judaeo-Christian teaching about the Fall and Eve's role within it did not give rise to this discrimination. It would be fair to conclude that male privilege and the denigration of women in

51

the Church is just our cultural version of how things pan out for women the world over. It would also be reasonable for Christian theologians, seeing global evidence for the subjugation of women, to assume that this bears out the inherent message of the story of the Fall – because of this, woman's desire is for her husband, but he lords it over her – and thus go on to assume that *this is how God ordained that it should be.*

In Chapter 6, 'Women and men in the new creation', we'll be thinking not only about the significance of Christ's great work of reconciliation and redemption with specific reference to the curse of Eve at the Fall, but also at the counter-culture option for equality we see in the gospels and the writings of St Paul. Both Jesus and Paul stood up for women and treated them with respect. Their attitudes belong to the *shalom*, the peace or harmony of Christ's kingdom as it began to take shape in the early church. Somehow, what they began got lost. What happened? Certainly the Roman Empire granting freedom of faith to the Church under Emperor Constantine made a big difference, because this change lowered the boundaries of cultural separation between the Roman Empire and the Church, and as we shall see in Chapter 5, 'Women in church history', the infiltration of Roman influence became a driving force for change in ecclesiastical attitudes to women.

But for now let's look at how, as the Church developed and established, the story of the Fall – and specifically the curse of Eve – was used as a proof text to justify misogyny. It is an object lesson in the inherent dangers of reading the Bible in this way, not holistically and with due regard for the meta-narrative, but plucking out verses and incidents as if by themselves they contained the whole story. Often the Bible is referred to as if it were a manual for living; if you want to know what it teaches about, for example, debt, you look up 'debt' in a concordance and find the verses that mention debt. If you want to know what it teaches about the place of women in the Church, you do the same thing. But it seems to me the Bible can be more usefully consulted like a map than like a manual. What is of crucial importance is the direction of travel rather than the static moments. Where is it heading? Where is it leading us? From where is it moving on and where is it going next?

A good example of this is the story of the binding of Isaac in Genesis 22. To appreciate the full force of this story for those to whom it was first told, it's important to know that Judaism originally emerged from Canaanite culture and religion, which included sacrifice of one's firstborn to placate the gods. If you read the story through the lens of people who until recently expected to sacrifice a child, then moved on from that practice, you begin to grasp its power. Here is *God* telling Abraham to sacrifice his son – thus jeopardizing the whole future of the Judaistic heritage. We watch the slow, reluctant journey on foot to Mount Moriah looming ominously in the distance. The boy carries the wood on his back. At a certain point, the servants are left behind; Abraham and Isaac trudge on alone together. The boy asks his father, where is the sacrifice? Abraham says God will provide. They climb the mountain. They build the altar. They prepare, laying the fire and making ready the knife. Abraham binds his son and lays him on the altar, and takes the knife to slay him. At *the last minute* the angel appears to stay his hand. A ram is provided for the sacrifice instead.

If we imagine this story being told around the campfires of the children of Israel, with drama, drawing out the long slow dread of the journey, the heart-in-mouth moment as the knife is raised, we begin to understand its potency in establishing the movement forward from sacrificing children to animal sacrifice. This story is overflowing with rich meaning; Christians later return to it in considering the sacrifice of Jesus. It speaks to us of Abraham's absolute faith and trust; it tells of the willingness to abandon oneself entirely to divine providence – there is so much here. But certainly one thing it does is move the understanding of the Jewish people on to the next level. It enables them to leave child sacrifice behind. It places in their hands not a proof text but a story. Stories develop understanding; proof texts don't.

In similar wise we see the story in Acts 10 and 11 of Peter moving on from seeing the Gentiles as outsiders, beyond the pale, different, to realizing that *they too* belong to God, that the family of faith is bigger than his imagination had room for. Indeed, one of the literary accomplishments of Luke the Evangelist is to trace the trajectory of faith story as the Church grows. If we take the Gospel of Luke and the book of Acts together as a pair, we can follow the expansion. In the Gospel of Luke, Jerusalem is central[1], with the Temple as its heart. In each of the Gospels, the evangelist uses the first words Jesus speaks to set out his stall thematically. In Luke, we first hear Jesus speak as a child to his parents in the Temple at Jerusalem: 'How is it that you sought me? Did you not know that I must be in my Father's house?'[2] And Luke's Gospel ends in the Temple at Jerusalem: 'And they returned to Jerusalem with great joy, and were continually in the temple blessing God.'[3]

The book of Acts starts in the same place: 'he charged them not to depart from Jerusalem, but to wait for the promise of the Father,'[4] with a group of Jewish men huddled together in the aftermath of strange events, waiting to see what will happen. With them, we see this great movement take flight, enlarging and expanding to embrace the Gentiles, growing beyond any and all expectation, with the outpouring of the Spirit 'on all flesh'[5], in an avalanche of inclusive love and faith.

Luke takes us onward and outward on the missionary journeys of Paul, and when the book of Acts finally comes to rest, it has travelled from Jerusalem, the heart of the Jewish world, to Rome – the heart of the secular Gentile world.

None of this is captured in proof texts; it can only be perceived by paying attention to the grand movement of the people of God under

---

1 For example, compare the temptation narratives in Luke with those in Matthew, and look at the centrality of the Temple in the early chapters.

2 Luke 2.49 RSV

3 Luke 24.52–53 RSV

4 Acts 1.4 RSV

5 Acts 2.17 (RSV), from Joel 2.28

the power of the Spirit – by treating the Bible more as a manual than a map and tracing the direction of travel.

I think this is where the great theologians of the church made their fatal mistake regarding the place and inclusion of women. They looked to proof texts in the scripture, instead of following the flow and the current of what God was doing there in the unfolding story of the people of God.

Let's look at what happens when the church fathers concentrate on the curse of Eve as a proof text justifying misogyny.

We begin first with the teaching of Paul, and will come back to that later because there was so much more to his attitude to women than this:

> A woman should learn in quietness and full submission. I do not permit a woman to teach or to assume authority over a man; she must be quiet. For Adam was formed first, then Eve. And Adam was not the one deceived; it was the woman who was deceived and became a sinner.[6]

> I want you to realize that the head of every man is Christ, and the head of the woman is man, and the head of Christ is God.[7]

> For man did not come from woman, but woman from man; neither was man created for woman, but woman for man.[8]

We can trace in the writings of Paul so much that affirms and advocates for gender equality, but that can be conveniently ignored once we have these verses to use as proof texts. Once the letters of Paul are incorporated into the canon of Scripture, they strengthen the story of the Fall to assist the entrenchment of misogyny. Here are some

---

6   1 Timothy 2.11–14 NIVUK

7   1 Corinthians 11.3 NIVUK

8   1 Corinthians 11.8–9 NIVUK

excerpts from the teaching of the church fathers on the place and nature of women:

> The very consciousness of [women's] own nature must evoke feelings of shame.[9]

> Woman is a temple built over a sewer.[10]

> In pain shall you bring forth children, woman, and you shall turn to your husband and he shall rule over you. And do you not know that you are Eve? God's sentence hangs still over all your sex and His punishment weighs down upon you. You are the devil's gateway; you are she who first violated the forbidden tree and broke the law of God. It was you who coaxed your way around him whom the devil had not the force to attack. With what ease you shattered that image of God: Man! Because of the death you merited, even the Son of God had to die... Woman, you are the gate to hell.[11]

> The woman taught once and ruined everything. On account of this let her not teach. The whole female race transgressed; let her not however grieve. God has given her no small cancellation, that of childbearing.[12]

> Woman was merely man's helpmate, a function which pertains to her alone. She is not the image of God but as far as man is concerned, he is by himself the image of God.[13]

---

9 Clement of Alexandria, Christian theologian (c150–215) Pedagogues II, 33, 2

10 Tertullian 'the father of Latin Christianity' (c160–225)

11 Tertullian

12 John Chrysostom, Archbishop of Constantinople, 349–407 CE

13 Augustine, Bishop of Hippo Regius (354–430)

If we continue to trace the thread after the Dark Ages and the establishment of Roman Christianity, we see this continued and intensified (see Chapter 5 for reference to the persecution of women by the Inquisition from the fifteenth century onward):

> Woman is a misbegotten man and has a faulty and defective nature in comparison to his. Therefore she is unsure in herself. What she cannot get, she seeks to obtain through lying and diabolical deceptions. And so, to put it briefly, one must be on one's guard with every woman, as if she were a poisonous snake and the horned devil. ... Thus in evil and perverse doings woman is cleverer, that is, slyer, than man. Her feelings drive woman toward every evil, just as reason impels man toward all good.[14]

> As regards the individual nature, woman is defective and misbegotten, for the active force in the male seed tends to the production of a perfect likeness in the masculine sex; while the production of woman comes from a defect in the active force or from some material indisposition, or even from some external influence.[15]

> Woman was made to be a help to man. But she was not fitted to be a help to man, except in generation, because another man would prove a more effective help in anything else.[16]

> The word and works of God are quite clear, that women were made either to be wives or prostitutes.[17]

---

14 Albertus Magnus, Dominican theologian, thirteenth century

15 Thomas Aquinas, Doctor of the Church, thirteenth century

16 Aquinas

17 Martin Luther, Reformer (1483–1546)

Thus the woman, who had perversely exceeded her proper bounds, is forced back to her own position. She had, indeed, previously been subject to her husband, but that was a liberal and gentle subjection; now, however, she is cast into servitude.[18]

Even as the church must fear Christ Jesus, so must the wives also fear their husbands. And this inward fear must be shewed by an outward meekness and lowliness in her speeches and carriage to her husband. . . . For if there be not fear and reverence in the inferior, there can be no sound nor constant honour yielded to the superior.[19]

The second duty of the wife is constant obedience and subjection.[20]

Such teaching and attitudes have persisted into modern times, with change hard-won and slow in coming. The Roman Catholic priesthood is still a male preserve and not until 1994 did the Church of England permit the ordination of women – and with much sensitivity and understanding towards the virulent opposition expressed. The first ordination of a woman as a bishop in the Church of England was not until 2015. In (relatively) modern times, one of the most potent images of the church's misogyny was the occasion when, in 1988, Billy Graham's daughter Anne Graham Lotz addressed the Southern Baptist Convention; the men all turned their backs on her, turned their chairs around.

John Wesley, no doubt influenced by his mother Susanna who pastored and presided over worship for her large household staff and family, spoke as something of a lone voice in this chorus:

---

18 John Calvin, Reformer (1509–1564)

19 John Dod, *A Plaine and Familiar Exposition of the Ten Commandements*, a Puritan book first published in 1603

20 Ibid

It has long passed for a maxim with many that 'women are only to be seen but not heard.' And accordingly many of them are brought up in such a manner as if they were only designed for agreeable playthings! No, it is the deepest unkindness; it is horrid cruelty; it is mere Turkish barbarity. And I know not how any women of sense and spirit can submit to it.[21]

Wesley, incidentally, was the first to license a woman (Sarah Crosby, in 1761) to preach within the Methodist movement and went on from that to license several more women preachers.

So there are from time to time dissenting voices, but in the long history of the church's oppression and silencing of women, we see again and again appeals to the curse of Eve. Because Adam listened to Eve and was persuaded to share the fruit she ate, all women should be shamed into silence forever, as untrustworthy wellsprings of sin. Because Eve fell and Adam followed, never again shall she be allowed to lead. This has developed into an exaggeration (or invention) of women's responsibility in all circumstances where she is mistreated. If a woman is raped, it must be because she was out and about late at night or had been drinking or was dressed immodestly. If she is beaten, she must have provoked the attack. The archetype of the evil temptress drawing the man into sin persists to this day. The strength and confidence admired in men are stridency and aggression when women exhibit them. It all tracks back to the story of the Fall and the curse of Eve and, crucially, to our use of it as a proof text to establish perpetuity, rather than as a starting point to remember but from which to move on.

The changes in recent times tend to be not so much the result of new illumination in our reading of the Bible as the result of pressure from secular culture, in which religious influence is diminishing, and an increasing tendency to see the Bible as an interesting collection of historical texts rather than as a sacred encounter with the

---

21 John Wesley's sermon *On Visiting The Sick* 1786

Spirit of God. In those parts of the church still holding to the Bible as the determinant of daily practice, a strong culture of male privilege is still intentionally in place.

The key to escaping from this culture of oppression without losing reverence for the Scriptures lies in a holistic reading of the Bible that takes account of the whole arc of sacred story, *starting* with the book of Genesis but not *stopping* there.

The responsibility Christians bear for the treatment of women in our society is not exclusive but is immense. The outlook of the church fathers, the monastic movement and the Romanization of the Church formed not only the culture of the household of faith, but of all Western civilization until around the time of the 1970s, at which point a cultural shift began and the cultural dominance of the Church began to tail off.

It is impossible to read with insight and understanding the great poets and playwrights of Western civilization unless one has familiarity with the Christian Scriptures and with the Mass. Such understanding of it is essential; without it one cannot grasp the nuances and resonances woven into the social, and therefore the literary, texture of our culture.

The effects of how the faith story in the Scriptures was read and understood have shaped social culture wherever in the world the gospel has travelled. So the writings of the church fathers on the heritage of the curse of Eve did more than merely determine a theological outlook. This teaching, spreading out through the monasteries and the parishes and the missions, meant that until 1891 an English man was legally entitled to beat his wife, until late 1918 English women had no political vote, until 1925 the custody of children in case of divorce was the father's right, until 1975 an English woman could not obtain a mortgage without a male guarantor, until 1991 marital rape was not recognized as a possibility in England.

A man 'giving away' a woman to another man on her wedding day is part of this cultural legacy. So is the commonly persisting assumption that in a family where both spouses work outside the home, the woman is responsible for child care, house cleaning and providing food. Likewise, the practice of a woman adopting her husband's surname rather than her own upon marriage is still almost universal. The whole social and legal principal of Coverture[22] grew out of Roman cultural norms spreading to France and thence to England with the Norman Conquest, and these same Roman norms melded with the theology of the developing church and in turn shaped the development of all Western culture.

One often hears the argument that discrimination against women cannot be a problem when the women themselves support it – when Christian women proudly uphold the headship of men, when women assume that the care of children and the home is their job and husbands are 'good' or 'helping' if they share responsibility. But of course, cultural norms influence and shape the women of the culture as well as the men, even when the results are detrimental to them.

Questioning our own assumptions, and moving on from the cultural perspectives through which we have seen the world, is inevitably slow. It is only step by step that such paradigms change. With regard to the place of women in society, it is not theological enlightenment but secular cultural forces that are driving change. Even so, once change begins, so do questions; emerging from the grip of unchallenged assumptions, we start to see life differently. Then a new theological framework starts to form. We begin to read the Scriptures differently.

Before we move on . . .

let's reflect.

1 What were your responses to the views on women expressed by the church fathers? Did their attitudes surprise you, or were they very

---

22 Coverture – the doctrine/principle of law whereby a woman's rights and obligations were subsumed into her husband's upon marriage.

familiar? What has been your own experience of the role of women in the Church, and the attitudes of church leaders towards women?

2 What are your own thoughts about the relationship of men and women in society and in the Church? Do you feel strongly about binary sexuality and gender (clear division of appearance and role between men and women)? How do you respond to modern society's increasing acceptance of gender fluidity?

3 What are your thoughts about women in church leadership? How do you respond to the great care with which the Church seeks to pastor and accommodate those for whom the introduction of women leaders is a deep offence? It is often said that in the struggle for equality there have been both wounds and cause for repentance on both sides; how do you feel about that?

4 As you consider your personal thoughts and feelings about the social and ecclesiastical roles assigned to men and to women, both in times past and in the present day, can you trace the formation and development of your own attitudes? Who influenced your outlook? How, and to what extent, has this changed with life experience? In what ways do you think your views might still change on this subject? What are your unanswered questions?

5 Do you detect any conflict within yourself over these matters? Is there any aspect where your upbringing or instincts are at odds with your intellectual frame of reference? Thinking of your own relationships with men and with women, do you notice significant differences in how you speak to them and behave towards them? If you do, can you feel your way to your motivations?

And let's move on, now, to thinking about some prominent female theologians, starting with the Dark Ages and moving on to the late Middle Ages, by which time the ideas of the church fathers, the monastic movement and the influence of Roman culture had contributed to the place of women in the Church.

5

Women in church history

What we see is what we get

In the story of the Fall, we see the snake telling Eve she will not die, as
God said, if she eats the fruit of the tree, but her eyes will be opened
to discern good from evil. As soon as Eve begins to envisage and
embrace this idea, it starts to take place – she sees that the fruit of
the tree is good. What we envisage and conceptually embrace shapes
and determines whatever circumstances life has given us; you can
give two different people the same set of circumstances, and they
will bring out of them a different result, because they envisage them
differently.

How Jesus envisages his faith community is how it is going to
be. Jesus is the Messiah, the Christ, the Monad[1], the Only Son of
God. He stands in perfect alignment with divine power and will, the
channel of the Holy Spirit in all the Spirit's creative power. He speaks
of his followers as belonging to the vine: a living entity[2]. Paul takes
the idea a stage further, envisaging the faith community (that would
one day be the Church) as a body[3]. Not a hierarchy, not an institution, not an army or an organization – a body. A living one.

A body, a living organism, can be healthy or unhealthy, and good
health in a body is achieved by maintaining balance. All illness is, at
root, imbalance, and healing is best addressed holistically. If balance
is restored in the body, healing results, peace re-establishes. This is
true of the body of Christ in the Church. Its most toxic pockets have

---

1   In Pythagorean philosophy, the first or supreme metaphysical being, the dot at the
    centre of the radiating and enveloping circle of life.

2   John 15.

3   Ephesians 1.22–23; 1 Corinthians 12.12–13; Romans 12.3–5; Colossians 1.24.

been those where power concentrates and accumulates, where status and its attendant jealousies intensify, where the masses turn a blind eye to predation upon the vulnerable by those given power. In these toxic pockets, the Church rots, and people suffer. It can be healed only by restoring balance. Once the accumulations of power and status disperse, *shalom* can return.

A great turning point in the Church's life came at the Synod of Whitby, when King Oswiu changed the course of Christian faith practice in the British Isles.

Columba's monks who evangelized Britain from Iona introduced the gospel with wisdom and gentleness. They worked with the spirituality of the receiving culture shaped around the agricultural year. They settled the deep fast of Advent alongside the season of No-Time following the end of the year at Samhain (beside which they settled All Hallows and All Souls). They settled the feast of the Incarnation alongside the winter solstice festival of Yul (the turn, the birth of the infant light). They settled the purification of the Virgin Mary alongside Imbolc, Brigid's tide, the time of cleansing, and called it Candlemas – at this time the ancient Celts met the returning light with candles lit in every house, and the monks worked with that. This season of purification began the fast of Lent, when it made sense to let the hens have their eggs for hatching and the cattle keep their milk for their young, and eat vegetables. They settled the feast of the resurrection on the celebration of fertility and new life at the vernal equinox festival of Ostara, that became Easter, Christ emerging from the womb of the earth in risen joy. Pentecost with the arrival of the Spirit in wind and fire settled in beside the fire festival of Beltane. At the summer solstice, they placed the feast of St John the Baptist close to the summer solstice festival of Litha at the zenith of the year; John, whom Jesus called the greatest in the kingdom of heaven, points down the year to the infant Christ who will come in the darkest days and reminds us to make the most of the light while it is in the world. On Lugnasadh, when the barley harvest started the season of reaping, the monks settled Lammas, thanksgiving for the bread of life. As the harvest concluded with everything safely gathered in at the autumn equinox festival of Mabon, the monks introduced the feast of St Michael and All Angels – the reapers, reminding us that death is coming and calling us to get ready. The year concluded with the mysterious observance of Samhain, the time of remembrance and veneration of the ancestors, before the year held its breath in No-Time, awaiting the return of the light.

So the early Celtic church worked with the seasons of the light and the rhythms of the agricultural year, establishing the gospel in the hearts and minds of the people, baptizing their understanding into the Christian faith. The Synod of Whitby changed all that.

Into the primarily Celtic Christianity of Northumbria had come a growing Roman influence, including Bishop Wilfrid and King Oswiu's Queen Eanfled. As Roman practice developed alongside Celtic practice, a problem arose over the dating of Easter. King Oswiu, who followed the usage of Iona, celebrated Easter on a different day from Queen Eanfled who followed Roman practice, and the church needed a unified consensus on when exactly to celebrate this crowning feast of the ecclesiastical year, because it was causing division in the royal household.

At the Synod of Whitby, Bishop Colman spoke for the Iona custom and Bishop Wilfrid for the Roman, with King Oswiu basing his judgment in the end on the deciding factor that St Peter was given by Jesus the keys of heaven and was the rock upon which the Church was built. He then – with humility, for his own practice had followed that of Iona – conceded that proper authority lay with the Petrine (Roman) tradition and thus delivered the British church into the shaping of Roman influence, which was substantially different from the Celtic.

The Emperor Constantine's granting of freedom of religion to Christians in the revolutionary Edict of Milan in CE 313 in effect spearheaded the intertwining of Roman law with canon law, resulting in the development of the Church into a cultural proponent of the Roman Empire. Roman legal structures and vocabulary began to shape the Church. The original common life of the Church, with its citizenship of heaven[4] rather than of earth, and its rendering unto Caesar[5] what belongs to Caesar (money) and unto God what belongs to God (the human soul), and its standing firm on the principle of neither male nor female, slave nor free in Christ[6], morphed into an acceptance of the Roman culture of paterfamilias exercised through a male priesthood in apostolic succession.

But before Roman Christianity was adopted as the cultural mould of the Church in the British Isles, we catch a glimpse of an alternative point of view.

Hilda of Whitby, 614–680

The Synod of Whitby was held at Abbess Hilda's double monastery Streanæshalch (or Streonshalh), later known as Whitby Abbey.

Hilda was an outstanding example of the possibility and practice of female leadership in the Church.

She was profoundly influenced in childhood by the example of Aethelburh of Kent, the second wife of King Edwin of Northumbria, Hilda's great uncle. Aethelburh agreed to marry the pagan Edwin only on condition that she be allowed to continue practicing the Christian faith rather than following the traditional path of adopting her husband's religion. The outcome of this was the conversion of Edwin and the baptism of his whole household – including the 11-year-old Hilda – in a little wooden chapel built for the purpose, near where York Minster stands today.

Aethelburh's example made a deep impression on Hilda, who

---

4   See John 18.36, John 17.14, Philippians 3.20, 1 Peter 2.9, Colossians 3.2-3, etc.

5   Matthew 22.15-21

6   Galatians 3.28

20 years later became a Christian nun. First in Hartlepool, then in Whitby, she established a 'double monastery': one half for nuns, the other for monks. She led with skill and energy and laid particular emphasis on properly educated clergy and biblical study.

An educated woman of great vision and breadth of mind, Hilda was renowned for the peaceable justice of her governance, for skilled administration and inspired teaching, and for encouraging and developing the gifts of others – most famously the cow-herd Caedmon who, under her influence at Whitby, became England's first Christian poet. Hilda was revered and loved for her inclusive spirit and her concern for the poor and the oppressed.

Hilda highly prized leadership formation – no less than five bishops owed their training to Whitby Abbey, and kings and commoners alike came to seek her advice and wise counsel. Under her leadership, Whitby Abbey became a centre of excellence, fostering study of arts and sciences, collecting an impressive library, deepening devotion, and developing craftsmanship as well as academic prowess.

A measure of her spiritual stature was the humility and grace with which she accepted King Oswiu's edict that England should follow Roman Christian practice. It was not her preference, nor in her judgement the right choice, but she used her influence to ensure its peaceful acceptance.

What a startling contrast Hilda's seventh-century Abbey at Whitby offers to the suspicion with which intelligent and outspoken women were later held between the mid-sixteenth to mid-eighteenth centuries, when female education and independence of mind were regarded as witchcraft and led to wise women being burned at the stake on a massive scale – thousands upon thousands.

Hildegard of Bingen, 1028–1179

Abbess Hildegard also presided over a double monastery. The tenth child of an affluent family, she was very devout and given to visions (in modern times thought possibly to be migraine-associated hallucinations). She was placed as an eight-year-old child in a 400-year-old Benedictine foundation at Disibodenberg, enclosed with Jutta, an anchorite attached to the community, who later became *magistra*[7] of the young women that families continued to place under her care. Hildegard avidly availed herself of the opportunities for study in this situation, herself became a nun at 15 years old, and when Jutta died in 1136 (30 years after Hildegard's arrival), Hildegard succeeded her as *magistra* by unanimous vote.

Her particular situation gave her less freedom of administration than Abbess Hilda enjoyed – at Disibodenberg, Hildegard was under the authority of the presiding abbot. The early years of her vocation were spent in nursing and manuscript illumination, but she continued to experience visions which – with a certain amount of hesitation – she began to write down once she held the position of superior of the women's house. In 1141, when Hildegard was 43, she shared her visions with her confessor, and they were submitted to the Archbishop of Mainz to have their authenticity weighed, and a theological committee judged them to be authentically inspired.

At this point Hildegard began to grow into the stature of her real self and assert her point of view. Her writing continued and flourished – in addition to further works of prophecy and visions, she wrote plays and lyric poetry set to music of her own composition, two treatises on medicine and natural history – including gynaecological information and advice – and lives of the saints. She also, just for fun, made up a language.

Living under male authority definitely chafed on Hildegard, and after twelve years as superior of the women's section at Disibodenberg, she began in 1147 to seek the freedom of an all-female foundation under her own leadership. This was not achieved without a struggle; her abbot opposed this proposal, and at one point

---

7   i.e. the superior, like an abbess of the women's section.

Hildegard took to lying rigid like a stone to demonstrate her immovability. They let her go. Her move to the women-only house at Rupertsberg was achieved by 1150. This foundation attracted many vocations, with as many as 50 members, and Hildegard founded a daughter house at Eibingen (still in existence).

As a leader, Hildegard's style had a certain cheery and creative flair. The wealthy women who came to share the religious life brought their jewellery, which they continued to wear – this was honouring to God, she said, not vain display.

In her sixties she began to travel, teaching in Benedictine monastic meetings and also as a public speaker. Of noble birth and enjoying considerable status and renown, with an outlook decidedly her own, Hildegard had no hesitation in speaking her mind. She corresponded with Henry II of England and his wife Eleanor of Aquitaine, as well as Emperor Frederick Barbarossa and the Archbishop of Mainz – both of whom she challenged in her letters. In her eighties she had a serious run-in with the ecclesiastical authorities for allowing the burial of an excommunicated aristocrat in sanctified ground at her monastery. She argued the validity of this course of action with some force, insisting that God had personally instructed her to do it, but the church authorities ordered the body to be exhumed and taken away. So Hildegard concealed the whereabouts of the grave, whereupon the authorities excommunicated her entire community and told them they had to stop singing. Hildegard strongly objected to this and appealed to higher authority, eventually succeeding in getting the interdict lifted.

When we look at her life as a whole, we see a joyous, creative, fearless, spirited approach, with a celebration of beauty and femininity. In her writings Hildegard personified spiritual aspects as female figures – Sapienta, Carita and Ecclesia – and her work was accomplished, imaginative and complex.

What we are seeing in this time frame is considerable latitude still open to women of courage and determination within the structures of a church under masculine dominance. Hildegard has less freedom than Hilda of Whitby 500 years earlier, but nothing like the systematic persecution of the Inquisition is even in sight here.

Hildegard's turbulent relationship with authority meant the church declined to canonize her for a very long time. Not until 2012 was she declared a saint by Pope Benedict XVI and named as a Doctor of the Church (accrediting her teaching as church doctrine) later in that same year.

Dame Julian of Norwich, 1342–1416

Julian was an anchorite, following the rule of life[8] set out for anchorites and living according to their particular discipline enclosed in a small dwelling built onto the exterior of a church. One window opened onto the sanctuary for the anchorite to participate in the Eucharist, another onto the street so people could come to seek the hermit's counsel.

She was widely known and respected for her holiness of life and prophetic spirit and for her mystical visions which formed the basis of her book. She worked as a catechist and spiritual director and wrote the earliest surviving book in the English language of female authorship: *Showings of Love*, usually known as *Revelations of Divine Love*.

Julian is not the only medieval writer to bring to prominence the divine feminine, but her work is groundbreaking in the detail and particularity of her exploration of the feminine aspects of the holy Trinity and of God's relationship with humanity.

Julian associates Christ's role of salvation with the motherhood of God, saying, 'our Saviour is our true mother in whom we are

---

8 Early thirteenth century – known as *The Ancrene Riwle* or *The Ancrene Wisse* (in Middle English 'wisse' is knowledge or guidance – like 'wisdom' – and 'riwle' is the medieval spelling of 'rule'). There is speculation as to authorship but no certainty.

eternally born and by whom we shall always be enclosed.' She drew upon the tradition of connecting the Holy Spirit with the feminine figure of Wisdom (Sapienta), saying, 'God All-wisdom is our mother by nature' and 'the great power of the Trinity is our father, and the deep wisdom of the Trinity is our mother, and the great love of the Trinity is our lord'[9]. She went further out on a limb with her attribution of femininity to all three persons of the Trinity:

> I understand three ways of contemplating motherhood in God. The first is the foundation of our nature's creation; the second is his taking of our nature, where the motherhood of grace begins; the third is the motherhood at work . . . and it is all one love.

Though she uses plenty of masculine images for God, Julian is unusual (in her time perhaps unique) in not subordinating the feminine aspects, saying: 'as truly as God is our Father, so truly is God our Mother.'

Julian links specific aspects of motherhood – giving birth and suckling – with the salvific work of Christ[10], saying, 'And so Jesus is our true mother by nature, at our first creation, and he is our true mother in grace by taking on our created nature'[11], likening Christ's agony on the cross with the pain of childbirth, and then going on to say:

> So next he had to feed us, for a mother's dear love has made him our debtor. The mother can give her child her milk to suck, but our dear mother Jesus can feed us with himself, and he does

---

9   *Revelations of Divine Love* Ch.58

10 The very title of Julian's book, 'Showings' has connotations with childbirth. When labour begins, it can be marked by what was once called 'a bloody show', as the mucus plug sealing the entrance to the womb comes away. It is the herald of a new birth. Changing this to 'Revelations' is an unwitting but substantial change to the theological imagery.

11 Ch. 59

so most generously and most tenderly with the holy sacrament which is the precious food of life itself[12].

Her writing is also strikingly different from the norms of her contemporaries (and from Christian theological norms in all ages) in her treatment of the subject of sin. Julian – probably best known for saying, 'All shall be well, and all shall be well and all manner of thing shall be well' – took a kind and compassionate view of the sinful human condition, seeing it as something to be healed rather than punished. In her vision, Christ is there to save and restore us, not sternly or with an accusatory attitude, but gently:

> But often when our falling and our wretchedness are shown to us, we are so much afraid and so greatly ashamed of ourselves that we scarcely know where we can put ourselves. But then our courteous Mother does not wish us to flee away, for nothing would be less pleasing to him; but he then wants us to behave like a child. For when it is distressed and frightened, it runs quickly to its mother; and if it can do no more, it calls to the mother for help with all its might. So he wants us to act as a meek child, saying: My kind Mother, my gracious Mother, my beloved Mother, have mercy on me. I have made myself filthy and unlike you, and I may not and cannot make it right except with your help and grace. . . And then he wants us to show a child's characteristics, which always naturally trusts in its mother's love in well-being and in woe.[13]

This emphasis on fearless trust in the unfailing love of God, drawing on the image of motherhood, establishes Julian as a uniquely feminist theologian. In the time in which she lived, how did she get away

---

12 Ch.60

13 Ch.61

with this? The key to that is most likely her enclosure and her obscurity. Her freedom to write and teach are secured by the limitation of her anchor-hold and protected by the presentation of her theology as mystical visions (which is not to say her visions were no more than a literary device, merely that this form may have kept her safe from persecution).

Margery Kempe, 1373–1478

The daughter of a merchant (so, not of noble birth and not educated), Margery Kempe was a woman of intelligent mind and questing spirit. Her life was characterized by inner conflict and contradiction. She wrote the first English autobiography yet was herself illiterate. She was married and the mother of fourteen children, yet her mystical visions and compulsion to be a pilgrim (she ended up in Jerusalem, a long way from her home in Kings Lynn) drew her away from domestic responsibility. The unsettling manifestations of her religious devotion, in public displays of weeping, screaming and spiritual hysteria, caused many to regard her as insane and denigrate her as a fraud and a heretic – yet she had a considerable following, including members of the clergy, who regarded her as a true visionary.

Though she could neither read nor write, Margery listened to books read out to her – including works of Richard Rolle and Walter Hilton. Her pilgrimages were inspired by hearing the *Revelationes* of Brigid of Sweden who, like Margery, was the mother of a large family. Margery is particularly interesting in speaking with the voice of an under-represented section of society: married laywomen. *The Book of Margery Kempe* tells of her visionary and mystical experiences, her temptations, her pilgrimages and her trials for heresy. Though she was never convicted, Margery stood trial many times. She was accused of preaching without ecclesiastical approval and of Lollardy[14]. The church authorities disliked her habit of wearing white[15], the very public nature of her pronouncements and the disturbing manner in which she delivered them.

We see Margery as torn between her spiritual calling and the pragmatic realities of her life, experiencing tormented demonic visions after the birth of her first child, longing for celibacy yet tempted by sexual pleasure and established within a marriage, running businesses from home[16] yet yearning to turn from the world.

At the age of 40 she made a visit to Julian in Norwich, staying with her for some days. Julian received her kindly, approved her revelations and judged her spirituality to be genuine, but cautioned her to evaluate her contribution by how beneficial it might be to her fellow Christians. 'Carry on, but tone it down if you can,' seems to have been the thrust of Julian's advice.

The significance of Margery's life and work is generally held to be the remarkable insight it gives us into the life of a middle-class medieval woman, but for our purposes here, there is something more. In the late Middle Ages, theology, scriptural interpretation and preaching were strictly the prerogative of the male priesthood. The only avenue of theological exploration that remained open to women was mysticism. Perhaps Margery's extreme manifestations of devotion, though they made her seem seriously odd, were what kept her safe from accusation as she persisted in sharing her religious insights and understanding; they allowed her to identify not as a preacher but as a mystic. Yet she never stopped being a thorn in the flesh of the establishment. What is particularly interesting is to observe what aggravation Margery caused, how odious an offence she was to men in authority – whether ecclesiastical or civic. 'A cheating slut, a cheating Lollard and a cheating misleader of the people', the mayor of

---

14 The pre-Protestant religious movement begun by John Wycliffe.

15 The virginal costume of a nun.

16 A brewery and a grain mill, both of which failed.

Leicester called her and had her imprisoned. Later she was brought before the steward of Leicester Castle, and Margery sturdily insisted that she knew no Latin, which would have marked her out as one of those dangerous learned Lollard women. She was interrogated in English, and she gave detailed answer to their intense questioning, but was returned to prison. Later she was brought before the abbot, the canons, the dean and the mayor and after being questioned in even more detail than before, was able to establish her orthodoxy to their satisfaction. But on travelling to York she was in the same sort of trouble again with the religious authorities – and so it went on. And to justify their attempts to silence her, could not the men who ran the Church appeal to the support of Scripture as well as the weight of tradition? Was not the whole human race cursed because a man listened to a woman in the garden of Eden? Did not St Paul adjure women to remain silent, asking their husbands at home if they wanted to know anything?

Margery's real crime, as the silencing of opinionated women gained momentum in the fourteenth and fifteenth centuries, was to be a woman who would not shut up.

Also of interest is the trial of Joan of Arc in 1431 (when Margery Kempe was in her late fifties). Joan's cautious and astute answers to her inquisitors made it difficult for them to find any fault in her religious position. In the end she was sentenced to death because she would not renounce her visions and give up wearing men's clothing (the attire of a soldier, which she said she wore at God's command). Margery Kempe and Julian of Norwich were protected in their work as theologians by expressing their thoughts as mystical visions, but the difference in Joan of Arc's case was the wearing of male apparel. She repeatedly explained that her prison guards often attempted to rape her, and that wearing men's clothes tied tightly with cords was necessary to prevent their success – and her inquisitors were neither surprised nor distressed that this should be so. To insist upon wearing garments that prevented rape proved to be, for Joan, a capital offence.

Before we move on . . .

let's reflect.

1 How do you think about God? Do you find imagery helpful – like Dame Julian's picture of a hurt child running to its mother – or is your concept of the divine more abstract than that? How do you feel about anthropomorphic terms for God – 'King', 'Father', 'Mother', 'Lord', 'Shepherd', etc.? Are these helpful to you? Are they so familiar they no longer conjure up an image at all? What imagery would you choose for your own sense of the divine? What images have you come across that resonate positively for you?

2 How do you respond to the visionary experiences of the mystics? Is this a familiar experience for you in your own communion with God, or is it something you can only view from the outside? Have you ever had a vision? In what ways would you say you experience the presence of God?

3 Margery Kempe was a laywoman with a big family, but left them at home while she went on extensive pilgrimages. Perhaps unsurprisingly, the businesses she started both failed. How do you personally balance commitment to spiritual practice and devotion with your responsibilities to your family and earning a living? Is it easy or is there sometimes conflict for you?

4 Abbess Hilda, Hildegard of Bingen and Dame Julian were all monastics. Hilda presided over a double monastery, Hildegard opted for a women-only community and Julian was a solitary. What are your thoughts about intentional communities, monasticism and the life of a hermit? Have you ever been drawn to such disciplines of life? What part do solitude, simplicity and silence play in your own spiritual practice?

5 During the 1980s, inclusive language became prominent in church liturgy and translations of the Scriptures, with the intention of making women visible in the faith community. Since

then, an emphasis has emerged on church leaders asking themselves how to attract *men* to church life. What are your thoughts about the balance of the sexes in the faith community? Does it matter? Have we got it right? What do you think?

And let's move on, now, to thinking about the attitude to women we see in the New Testament, the work of Christ on the cross, and how the redemption of humanity affects our gender relationships.

6

Women and men in the new creation

How Jesus treats women

Symbolism and story form the language of faith because it deals with the realm of mystery and tries to capture what is unavailable to the senses. So the Scriptures and the liturgy have an inherent opacity, obscurity, to them[1] – they are always about something else. It's not that they aren't true, but that their truth refers to something you can only see peripherally; you sense it, you glimpse it, some of us say we know it in our heart's core while others only wish they did. It's hard to answer the derision of atheists because the most real thing about our faith is not available for inspection. It can be experienced, but only by living as if it were true – and, to be honest, not always even then.

This means the stories the evangelists tell in the four gospels *mean* something. They have included them in their gospels for a purpose. It's important to make clear that doesn't imply they are made up, never happened, aren't true. On the contrary, they are double-true; they both happened and also point to something profound and elusive beyond themselves. This is why we can find ourselves in the Scriptures – because the stories of what happened in the lives of these people are also, we discover, our stories. For this reason, biblical literalism and fundamentalism achieve the diametric opposite of what they set out to do. Intending to make faith the most important

---

1   Cf. 1 Corinthians 13.12 – 'For now we see in a mirror dimly, but then face to face. Now I know in part; then I shall understand fully, even as I have been fully understood.' – RSV

thing of all, they merely desiccate it, robbing it of its profundity and immense resonance by trying to nail it down to something *merely* historical and literal. All shell and no kernel.

If you look into the stories for the mysteries they contain, and you track their path through the Scriptures to discern their direction of travel, it is possible to discern from the Scriptures where faith is headed and align your own journey according to that guiding star.

Let's look, then, at what the New Testament can show us and suggest to us about gender roles and relationships in the new and living Way. So you don't get utterly sick of that phrase as we go along, I'd like to introduce to you a second one that may be less familiar. You will of course know the phrase 'Kingdom of God', and 'Christ's Kingdom', but in a book about lifting the curse of Eve, I'd prefer to avoid such uncompromisingly patriarchal terms. In the Dark Ages, in Old English, they had another phrase – they spoke of the 'reach of Christ'[2], the extent of his influence, the spread of what came under his sway, his realm, the spread of his reign. I like this phrase better than 'kingdom'; it incorporates the sense of contact and shelter, of being under Christ's wing and within touching distance. So, when I speak of 'the reach of Christ', that's what it means. Let's look at gender roles and relationships as they can be in the reach of Christ, under the power of his influence.

The best place to start is always the life of Jesus, to look at what he did and notice what he challenged and what he affirmed.

The very first thing we see in the life of Jesus offers a direct challenge to cultural and social assumptions about women. Before Jesus was even born, Luke tells of Mary going to visit her kinswoman

---

2   The Old English word *rīce*, from which via the Old French 'riche' we get our modern word 'rich', meant wealthy or powerful. The proto-Germanic word *kuningarīkiją* became *cyningrīċe* in Old English, which was a conflation of *cyning* (that became 'king') and *rīċe* – meaning power. So *cyningrīċe* meant 'kingdom', and developed into the Middle English *kingriche* or *kingric*. Thus the *rīċe* (reach) of a king was the extent of his power.

Elizabeth[3] – Mary is pregnant with Jesus and Elizabeth with John the Baptist. Each of these women has a cloud over her; Joseph wanted to quietly separate from Mary because of her pregnancy, and Elizabeth has been unable to conceive. In the context of their religious and social culture, each woman is tainted with shame because women were *for men*, to come to them as virgins and bear their children. So right at the beginning of the life of Jesus, we see a story of God countering the assumptions and expectations of the socio-religious culture, acting in favour of the women and blessing them. Joseph is warned by God in a dream not to abandon Mary, because the baby she has conceived is of the Holy Spirit. Elizabeth is vindicated as a woman[4] and also gets to be the one to pronounce her son's name (because her husband Zechariah has been struck dumb for arguing with an angel)[5]. When Mary and Elizabeth greet one another, Mary utters her wonderful prophetic song[6] announcing God's justice and mercy, the liberation of the poor and oppressed. Later in Luke's Gospel, when Jesus begins to teach and preach, we see him very much as Mary's son – his words have a striking resemblance to hers.

In this story God acts in favour of women who have been shamed and rejected, reinstating their honour, seeing them not only as individuals but as courageous and prophetic figures – characters of faith, strength and influence.

We can extend the reach of Christ by standing with minority groups against social oppression.

Between the infancy narratives and Jesus' adult ministry come two significant events: the time when Mary and Joseph lost the boy Jesus at the festival in Jerusalem and eventually found him in conversation with religious scholars in the Temple, and the first of

---

3   Luke 1.39ff

4   Luke 1.25

5   Luke 1.59

6   Luke 1.46ff

the signs recorded by John, when Jesus turns water into wine at the wedding at Cana.

Particularly interesting here is that we see Jesus beginning to reshape faith identity. He was born into a strongly tribal religion, where submission to family ties was a priority. Deference to his parents was required from him in the law of Moses, 'Honour your father and your mother'. Yet Jesus chooses to go his own way and fulfil his own path. When his worried parents reproach him for causing them so much anxiety, he says: 'How is it that you sought me? Did you not know that I must be in my Father's house?'[7] He redefines belonging away from blood connection to faith connection. Similarly at the wedding at Cana, when Mary approaches him to communicate the concern over the wine running out, he responds, 'O woman, what have you to do with me?' He *does* do something about the wine, but he *doesn't* do it as a favour to his mother – he resists absolutely the string-pulling of family connection. In so choosing, not only does Jesus open the possibility of kinship and belonging to all the marginalized and dispossessed, he also loosens the cultural strictures that oppress women as well as act in their favour. It's about the bigger picture. He will not fall in with any kind of nepotism because he is bringing in a greater vision of inclusion and reconciliation. In saying 'No' to Mary, he says 'Yes' to all womankind.

This larger vision is most clearly expressed by Mark in writing about the moment when Jesus' mother and brother came to take him in hand[8] because they thought he must be out of his mind:

> And his mother and his brothers came; and standing outside they sent to him and called him. And a crowd was sitting about him; and they said to him, 'Your mother and your brothers are outside, asking for you.' And he replied, 'Who are my mother

---

7   Luke 2.49 RSV

8   Mark 3.19–21

and my brothers?' And looking around on those who sat about him, he said, 'Here are my mother and my brothers! Whoever does the will of God is my brother, and sister, and mother.'[9]

For Jesus, belonging is defined by faith – choice and decision – not by birthright. Under this definition, to be the mother, the sister of Jesus is (must be) something a woman chooses for herself, rather than something she is powerless to influence because it is under the control of another person, a man.

Jesus did take his family responsibilities seriously. Even in his extreme suffering on the cross, he commended his mother into the care of the beloved disciple[10], who took her into his home from that day on; but even then his interpretation of family responsibility moves beyond the merely tribal – he did, after all, have brothers – to the establishment of an inclusive house of faith, freely chosen.

In his dealings with women, Jesus consistently blocks the tendency of established religion to diminish them and make them responsible for the actions of men. He disregards exclusion made on the grounds of uncleanness.

We can extend the reach of Christ by working to affirm inclusion and resisting tribalism in the Church[11].

We see him[12] deep in conversation with a Samaritan woman ostracized within her own community, her reputation presumably tainted by the string of men with whom she has consorted. The story makes quite clear, it's not that Jesus doesn't know about this nor that he approves disorderly personal relationships or doesn't care about such things, it's that he will not allow this to define her. She is a person with a choice; she is not defined by her relationships with men,

---

9   Mark 3.31–35

10   John 19.26–27.

11   For an excellent exploration of this topic, see Peter Selby's book *BeLonging, Challenge to a Tribal Church*, SPCK 1991, ISBN-10: 0281044899, ISBN-13: 978-0281044894.

12   John 4.4–26

and she is not defined by her status as a foreigner, a non-Jew. She is an individual, a living soul, to whom is held out the hope of the Holy Spirit welling up to eternal life at the core of her being.

We can extend the reach of Christ by consistently affirming the upwelling of the Holy Spirit *within*, and *from the centre of*, womankind, not merely *for* women from the centre of mankind.

We see Jesus with the woman taken in adultery[13], taking the course of action that saves her life. Again, what he says to her makes clear it's not because he is indifferent to such things; on the contrary, when he parts from her, he says, 'Go and sin no more.' But he rescues her from the harshness of discrimination that would subject her to a hideously brutal death in punishment for a crime in which she may have had no choice, no agency – she would not have been acculturated to refusing men.

What Jesus says to this woman – 'Has no one condemned you? . . . Neither do I condemn you' – resonates strongly with the words earlier in the same gospel of John:

> For God so loved the world that he gave his only Son, that whoever believes in him should not perish but have eternal life. For God sent the Son into the world, not to condemn the world, but that the world might be saved through him.[14]

We can extend the reach of Christ by standing with women in a world that exploits their vulnerability through trafficking, rape, institutionalized inequality and domestic exploitation.

We see Jesus responding to the pleas of a Syro-Phoenician (Gentile) woman to heal her demonized daughter[15]. This is a particularly interesting story in that it shows Jesus resisting his disciples'

---

13 John 8.1–11
14 John 3.16–17 RSV
15 Matthew 15.21–28

instinct to just chase the woman away because she's annoying; it also shows his strong sense of priority, 'I was sent only to the lost sheep of the house of Israel', and shows his willingness to listen to her – a woman and Gentile – and allow her to persuade him to her point of view. Again, we see Jesus treating a Gentile woman with exactly the same respect as he would treat a Jewish man, and the responses of his disciples (both here and in the case of the woman at the well) make it clear that Jesus is departing from cultural norms.

We can extend the reach of Christ by holding space for minority groups and making opportunities for their points of view to be heard.

Luke tells the interesting story of the woman with an issue of blood[16]. This story is also in Mark's and Matthew's Gospels, and has upon it Mark's hallmark of interpolating one story into another. In this case, Jesus is called to help when a 12-year-old girl has died. On the way to her house, a woman who has been bleeding 12 years touches the hem of his garment in faith, and she is healed. The girl who has died is at the age of the menarche and the woman with bleeding that won't stop may well be peri-menopausal. The woman has been bleeding the whole time the girl has been alive. Of significance for us here is that healing goes out from Jesus to the woman despite the fact that her condition makes her ritually unclean, and that Jesus is involving himself with these female persons in whose plight the topic of menstruation is brought to the fore. For Jesus, this is as much his concern as theirs. He does not distance himself from something so personally female, and the fact that healing went out from him when the woman touched his garment in effect calls into question the uncleanness of menstruation. I do not see how, in the light of the witness of this Gospel story from three Gospels including the earliest, the Church felt able

16 Luke 8.43–48, Mark 5.25–34, Matthew 9.20–22

to support so long the exclusion of women from the sanctuary on grounds of menstruation[17].

Jesus' resistance to the faith community's categorization of some people as unclean and exclusion of women is also seen in the story of the woman who bathed his feet with her tears[18].

We can extend the reach of Christ by ensuring that the Church is welcoming to the physical reality of women as well as of men – the women are welcome on their own terms, not only if they are able to adopt male characteristics and act as pseudo-men.

Perhaps the most compelling of all the Gospel accounts showing Jesus modelling a revolution in the treatment of women is the well-known story of Mary and Martha[19].

It is likely that Jesus was teaching a group of men, presumably his disciples and some others, and it is likely that the room in which he sat was off-limits to women because it was the gathering place for men. The appointed role for women in such circumstances was to provide hospitality: to wait on the men. Listening to the teacher and discussing the theology was strictly the prerogative of men. When Martha asked Jesus to rebuke Mary for gatecrashing this male pre-serve and joining the theology group, she had every expectation he would do so. Mary had crossed the boundary line shamelessly, and there must have been something in what she knew about Jesus that gave her the courage to do so. We can infer some precedent in the words and actions of Jesus that emboldened Mary to step over the lines of gender apartheid and join the theology group. That Jesus upheld and defended her choice is in the order of re-making the world.

---

17 E.g., the teaching of Dionysius of Alexandria (241 CE), Jerome (347–419 CE), Timothy of Alexandria (680 CE), Theodore of Canterbury (690 CE), Theodulf of Orléans (820 CE), the *Decretum Gratiani* of 1140 CE incorporated into the *Corpus Iuris Canonici* of 1234 and in force until 1916, and the *Codex Iuris Canonici* of 1917, and the abiding (though not ubiquitous) tradition of the Church.

18 Luke 7.36–50

19 Luke 10.38–42

We can extend the reach of Christ by ensuring the presence of women in the places where theology is formed.

Women and the work of St Paul

When we look at a person's life and work, sometimes we see what we expect to see instead of what is actually there. We interpret what's in front of us according to the view we have through the lens of our already existing perspective. Everything looks gloomy through our sunglasses.

I believe I see this process at work sometimes when I observe people responding to the work and writing of St Paul. He has a reputation for being misogynistic, which I personally think is undeserved. Remember, we are looking not for the isolated content of actual sayings to use as proof texts, but for the direction of travel – where Paul was headed in respect of his socio-religious culture in terms of gender attitudes. That's what will determine our direction of travel in respect of our own context.

In four particular areas I believe Paul advocated for the affirmation and inclusion of women on equal terms with men.

Paul's recognition of female church leaders

Paul worked with and respected and promoted the work of female church leaders[20]. To find the evidence of this, you have to do a certain amount of excavation around the greetings and lists of names attached to Paul's letters.

One such leader was Lydia of Thyatira[21]. Paul usually started his missionary work in a new place at the local synagogue. He finds Lydia in a group of women assembled at a riverside *proseuchē* (translated as

---

20 For further reading about women leaders in the New Testament, I particularly recommend the work of Marg Mowczko – find her online at <https://margmowczko.com>.

21 Acts 16.14–15

'place of prayer', the word typically used for a synagogue) just outside the city gates of Philippi. He did not wait for or look for male devotees, but was happy to begin sharing the gospel with this group of women. Lydia's business dealing in expensive cloth would have conferred high social status upon her, and may possibly have contributed to her leading role in this group. She also commands her household – there is no mention of her deferring to a husband – so when she receives the gospel, she is free to offer the missionaries hospitality and spread the good news to everyone in her household. The story of Lydia shows that women held independent positions of leadership respected by the apostles.

Another prominent churchwoman was Priscilla of Corinth[22]. Paul met Priscilla and Aquila at Corinth on his second missionary journey, when they had just moved there from Italy. He lived and worked with them for 18 months, and then they travelled with him to Ephesus. Priscilla and Aquila are mentioned six times in the New Testament, always together; on four occasions Priscilla's name comes before Aquila's, which suggests her ministry may have been especially esteemed. We know[23] this couple risked their lives for Paul, the local church met in their home, their ministry is held jointly and their leadership is shared. Priscilla and Aquila are co-workers in establishing and building up the Church. Priscilla has a teaching role on a basis equal to her husband's, with the authority to correct and instruct men – and we know this exactly because Paul recognizes and affirms it.

In the letter to the Romans we get a fleeting glimpse of Junia of Rome[24], a scriptural snippet that has been the source of a

---

22 Acts 18.24–26

23 Romans 16.3–5

24 Romans 16.3–7. In the RSV Junia is entirely absent and has been transformed into the male 'Junias', the male form of the name. The NRSV, by contrast, renders the passage: 'Greet Andronicus and Junia, my relatives who were in prison with me; they are prominent among the apostles, and they were in Christ before I was.'

disproportionate amount of controversy because Junia was both a woman and a prominent apostle – a combination that sits uneasily with the assumptions of some commentators. This greeting in Paul's letter makes it clear that he respected and acknowledged Junia's position of leadership.

We also meet Phoebe of Cenchreae in the letter to the Romans[25]. That she is a church deacon challenges suppositions that church leadership must have been male. In establishing new churches, the apostles followed the practice of appointing elders and a deacon from among the first (and therefore the most trained) converts. Deacons ranked below apostles and elders, but their leadership role implied authority as well as pastoral care. This would have been a permanent position in church governance for the purpose of ensuring stability and guarding against heresy. A deacon needed a good grasp of theology and a dependably trustworthy character. Paul commended Phoebe's ministry and commented on her generosity and encouragement – 'she has been a benefactor of many'. In passing, he also refers to Julia, mentioned not as a wife or sister but in her own right. Paul is seeing the women in the church as contributing something valuable as individuals in their own right, not merely as adjuncts of men or helpful at arranging flowers and making tea.

Euodia and Synteche make an appearance in the letter to the Philippians[26], where we read of them working alongside Paul to extend the reach of the gospel. He mentions them along with Clement in the same way as he elsewhere refers to Timothy and Epaphroditus, as his co-workers. The specifics are not spelt out, but he says they have 'struggled' alongside him. The word can also be translated as 'contended' alongside him, which implies a role as fellow apologists and missionaries.

---

25 Romans 16.1–2,15
26 Philippians 4.1–3

We come across Chloe of Corinth in the letter to the Corinthians[27], where the reference to 'Chloe's people' suggests that it was she who was Paul's point of contact. House churches were the New Testament norm, and Chloe may have led and hosted one such congregation. Evidently Paul listens to, and takes seriously, those Chloe sends to him with news of the local church.

Apphia of Colossae crops up in just a tiny phrase in the letter to Philemon[28] which, though it is personal in tone, is also addressed to a group of people – whom Paul presumably trusts to weigh in with influence regarding his requests concerning the slave Onesimus. Paul addresses the letter to all the church members as well as to Philemon – and also to first Apphia, then, separately, Archippus. He refers to his ministry colleague Timothy and 'brother', and addresses Apphia as 'sister'; this would suggest he considers her to hold equal status as a colleague in ministry.

In 2nd Timothy, we encounter Eunice and Lois of Lystra[29]. They are Timothy's mother and grandmother, and in commending the sincerity of Timothy's faith, Paul acknowledges the influence of these women. How many writers do you know who, in complimenting a male church leader for his work, draws attention to the influence of his mum and grandma? Yet that's exactly what the supposedly misogynist Paul does here!

Throughout the writings of St Paul we can trace respect and esteem for the Christian women alongside whom he worked and a readiness to affirm and acknowledge their contribution.

Paul worked for women to be taken seriously

Where Paul writes about women being quiet in church, covering their heads and giving them no authority to teach and preach, he is

---

27 1 Corinthians 1.10–12

28 Philemon 1.1–4

29 2 Timothy 1.5–7

often assumed to be misogynistic. But what if these are instances of Paul working to see that women were respected and taken seriously?

It is possible that in denying women authority to teach and preach[30], he is requiring them to work within cultural norms of what is realistic. We know that where he finds women (like Lydia) in positions of leadership, Paul affirms and does not try to silence them. Perhaps he is willing to accept the cautions of cultural norms, in the same way that he accepted circumcision for Timothy[31] even though he personally regarded it as an unnecessary and retrograde step[32]. We must acknowledge that this particular passage from 1 Timothy reads a little more emphatically than that, but even so, it should be taken together with the many places in the New Testament where we find Paul willing to work respectfully alongside women and not elevate it to special proof-text status of its own.

Where Paul speaks of women keeping silence in his section on church order in 1 Corinthians[33], it is unclear what kind of silence he means. Some commentators suggest Paul is referring not to teaching, prophecy or other verbal contribution to the gathering, but to conversation and calling out comments or questions in a manner he perceives as disruptive. This would make sense in the context of his arguing for peace and against disorder and urging them to have these discussions in private at home, not spontaneously in a public arena. The effect of this would be that women in church would be taken more seriously, not less, as self-controlled and mature individuals (like the men).

Paul's teaching on head covering in 1 Corinthians 11[34] seems to arise from decency and modesty issues associated with the long hair of women. He uses the word *peribolaion*, translated as 'covering'

---

30 1 Timothy 2.11–14

31 Acts 16.3

32 Galatians 2.3–5

33 1 Corinthians 14.33–35

34 1 Corinthians 11.2–16

in saying a woman's hair is given her for a covering. Paul may be making reference to the contemporary belief in the sexual potency of a woman's hair and therefore recommending she cover her hair for decency. This would be consistent with the Hippocratic understanding of hair as a vessel of sexual potency[35]. One cannot, in making this argument, overlook Paul saying that women proceeded from men not vice versa and so women should wear a sign of authority, but the whole passage is about order and decency, laying requirements upon men as well as women, and a moratorium on church leadership by women does not necessarily follow from it. In requiring church members to exhibit decorum and decency, avoiding scandal, Paul is paving the way for Christians and their gospel to be taken seriously in society, held in respect and giving no occasion for scandal.

Paul addressed male/female relationships in the domestic sphere

Ephesians 15 offers Paul's teaching on submission within marriage, and gives us a master class in how to work within existing cultural norms – just as the monks of Iona worked with the cultural norms of the British Isles in establishing the gospel there. He speaks of Christ as the head of his body the Church and a husband as head of his wife in marriage. He instructs wives to submit to their husbands as the Church submits to Christ. At first reading, this might seem to imply the domination of women by men and the subordination of women to men in domestic relationships. But closer attention to the text suggests something different. Paul also instructs husbands to love their wives as Christ – who was crucified, who laid down his life – loves his Church. And life only continues for a head as much as for a body when they remain united; neither can live without the other. What

---

35 Hairs were thought to be hollow tubes transmitting semen emanating from the brain. I know, I know – makes you wonder which of our own scientific beliefs will seem utterly bizarre one day, doesn't it?

Paul is recommending is *mutual* submission and harmony – union, not dominance.

When Paul directly addresses sexual relations within marriage, he speaks of being yoked together[36], which implies equality, and of not denying one another sexual intimacy[37] – he does not assume sexual intimacy is for a man to demand and a woman to yield up.

Paul's teaching about Christian marriage can be read to offer a picture of equality expressed in loving humility. We can observe in him a direction of travel away from male domination towards treating women with respect as equal partners. Certainly Paul is no twenty-first-century feminist, nor would it be reasonable to expect that of him, but within the context of his culture and heritage, we can observe a movement towards, not away from, equality. We see this most plainly and overtly in Paul's letter to the Galatians: 'There is neither Jew nor Greek, there is neither slave nor free, there is neither male nor female; for you are all one in Christ Jesus.'[38]

Christ's great work of reconciliation

In addition to being able to trace a movement towards inclusion and respect of women in the words and actions of Jesus and Paul, it is essential that we understand the significance for male/female relationships in the work of Christ on the cross.

In Christian theology, creation, incarnation, crucifixion, resurrection, ascension and outpouring of the Spirit at Pentecost combine together as essential components of the establishment of *shalom*, of Christ's reach on earth.

Man and woman were created and blessed equally in the image

---

36 2 Corinthians 6.14

37 1 Corinthians 7.3–4

38 Galatians 3.28 RSV

of God, as we have seen. In the Fall, their relationship was fatally unbalanced into dominion and servitude. Then came Christ, born of woman, modelling a healed relationship of respect and mutuality, moving us away from blood ties and tribalism towards an inclusive family of faith. In the crucifixion, we see the Temple veil torn in two[39] – implying the opening of the new and living Way, access into the holy presence of God established for *all* humanity. In the resurrection, we see a scarred Christ showing new life as a spiritual being. So it will be for all of us; we are scarred, life has wounded us – and yet, in Christ, we have come through, we have the chance to be made new, to be partakers of his risen life. In the ascension, we see humanity taken up into heaven, no longer separated from God but joined together by this artery of life, the presence of Christ in heaven. At Pentecost we see the outpouring of the Spirit on all flesh – the nascent sign of the reach of Christ, and the possibility of inclusive holiness. This is the new creation, of which Paul writes in 2 Corinthians 5, going on to say:

> All this is from God, who through Christ reconciled us to himself and gave us the ministry of reconciliation; that is, in Christ God was reconciling the world to himself, not counting their trespasses against them, and entrusting to us the message of reconciliation[40]

The letter to the Ephesians[41] also speaks of those who were disjointed and divided being made one, built together into a single living temple. The letter to the Colossians[42] takes up the same theme, expounding the work of Christ as an act of healing bringing about a

---

39 Matthew 27.51

40 2 Corinthians 5.18–19 RSV

41 Ephesians 2.13-22

42 Colossians 1.15-23

new creation, whereby all creation is reconciled to God, a new reign of peace being effected by Christ's death on the cross.

The New Testament proposes a whole new fabric of community, characterized by humility and peace, in which the scars of the past are not forgotten but incorporated as a badge of reconciliation in our risen body of life.

The curse of Eve is lifted in this new creation; women and men are free to begin again. Their difficult relationship is scarred by dominion and subservience, but the new and living Way of Christ offers the opportunity to cross over into healed and balanced union.

Before we move on . . .

let's reflect.

1 We have thought about Jesus and Paul working with and challenging cultural norms about women. Thinking now of our own churches and the society in which we live, where do you perceive the need still to proceed with sensitivity, promoting equality without unnecessary antagonism? And where do you feel we have a responsibility simply to speak truth to power in advocating for women who live under oppression?

2 What do you feel about the implications for multi-cultural relations? As we hold together the Christian communion over very wide cultural difference around the world, and as we relate with people of faith in different religions, where do you feel we should make an uncompromising stand for gender equality and where must we be sensitive towards those who see things differently?

3 How do you perceive the establishment of healing and unity in your own life? What difference does your own faith as a Christian make to your gender roles and relationships? Can you identify areas still unresolved for you or puzzling? Are there any unhealed wounds?

4 The women leaders of the New Testament mostly appear only in fleeting glimpses caught in greetings and lists that form a small part of Paul's letters. How do you think we might make more visible, in our teaching and study materials, this definite presence of female leadership in the early church?

5 Could you create a liturgy of blessing called 'Lifting the curse of Eve', to celebrate the return in Christ's new creation to harmonious gender balance?

And let's move on, now, to thinking about the new and living Way of Christ, and the challenge this offers to our established patterns of religion.

7

Religion and the living Way

A religion is an attempt (ambitious and doomed) to serve God and Mammon. It makes career pathways out of vocations, cordons off holy ground and encases it in buildings, regulates spiritual experience in systems of examination and accreditation, discriminates between clean and unclean people, and develops funds and structures of governance. It becomes a mechanism of dominion, and as it does so, it ossifies. The minute it begins to organize, it starts to die.

A religion can be as dead and empty as a Chinese cabinet in a glass case in a museum – a sophisticated and complex designed structure of ingenious compartments, some evident and some locked and hidden and hard to discover and access. Or, caught at an earlier stage, it can be more organic and ongoing – like an ant-hill, then later like a beehive organized for commercial opportunity.

Humanity is inherently social, and worldwide its activities exhibit the instinct not only to dominate but also to colonize. It is an *opportunistic* dominance. Nowhere is this more clearly expressed than in the spread of religions. It is certainly evident in the Church, as we see what starts as 'beloved, let us love one another, because love is from God'[1] morph into 'acquiesce or we will burn you alive.'

A religion establishes a priesthood and tethers those who are in it to the institution by linking housing and financial remuneration to credal orthodoxy.

A religion cannot be merciful because it is not alive. It is a thing. It cannot accommodate difference: that's the point of it – to mould conformity.

---

1   1 John 4.7 NRSVA

The living Way of Jesus is not a religion. It is inherently transformative, and you cannot pin it down. In the words of Jesus: 'The wind blows where it wills, and you hear the sound of it, but you do not know whence it comes or whither it goes; so it is with every one who is born of the Spirit.'[2] It is possible to find the children of God, those who are born again and walking in the new and living Way, within the Church as well as outside of it, but it is not possible to contain or confine the Spirit that makes them what they are. You can't bottle it. You can't patent it. You can't monopolize it. Whatever else the Spirit of God may be, it is certainly and incontrovertibly free. It always will be, and there is nothing anyone can do to change that:

Now the Lord is the Spirit, and where the Spirit of the Lord is, there is freedom.[3]
    If you continue in my word, you are truly my disciples, and you will know the truth, and the truth will make you free ... So if the Son makes you free, you will be free indeed.[4]

In the Church we can plainly see the mechanism of religion. We can see men farming women like ants farming greenfly, securing paternity and domestic service from love. We can see mission expressed as a reign of terror and oppression, inflicting unspeakable torture upon any who would not comply and be bent into subservience. But we can also trace the living Way of Jesus. In any generation we can observe the veins of kindness, mercy and grace, carrying the lifeblood of faith, the healing of *shalom*.

Jesus said, 'I am the Way, the Truth and the Life,'[5] and this always

---

2 John 3.8 RSV

3 2 Corinthians 3.17 RSV

4 John 8.31-32, 37 RSV

5 John 14.6 RSV

new and living Way is there as a kind of parallel universe to the structures of religion. At any moment a person can choose to take off the straightjacket of religion and don the white garment of Christ, the flow and freedom of the new and living Way. Whenever someone chooses to, they can leave the musty confinement of the closed structure of religion and set out on the new and living Way, which cannot be confined or defined because it is a direction of travel, it is creative not created, it is alive.

This is like the difference between a creature with an exoskeleton and one with an internal skeleton. Religion has an exoskeleton, containing life within the rigidity of its structures. The Way of Jesus is not without form or discipline, but when you touch it, it is soft; when you encounter it, you meet kindness. Its discipline is within, at its core. The Way of Jesus takes responsibility, where a religion imposes regulation. That's what the word means, in the Latin *religare*, 'to bind fast'.

There is a picture of this in the story of the raising of Lazarus in John's Gospel:

> So they took away the stone . . . [Jesus] cried with a loud voice, 'Lazarus, come out.' The dead man came out, his hands and feet bound with bandages, and his face wrapped with a cloth. Jesus said to them, 'Unbind him, and let him go.'[6]

Religion is not real; it is invented. The new and living Way of Jesus *is* real. There is a tendency to confuse the two; when statisticians track church attendance and census records of those who identify as Christian, it is possible to misunderstand and believe the Way of Jesus can be measured, evaluated, monitored and quantified because we can do those things with the various forms of ecclesiastical institution. But in fact it is not possible to carry out such exercises

---

6   John 11.41, 43-44 RSV

upon the new and living Way. It is always new, always alive, always there – the only choice is whether to follow it, plunge in, participate, or not. You can detect it, but you cannot understand it unless you participate. This is what the story of the healing of blind Bartimaeus teaches us:

> And they called the blind man, saying to him, 'Take heart; rise, he is calling you.' And throwing off his mantle he sprang up and came to Jesus. And Jesus said to him, 'What do you want me to do for you?' And the blind man said to him, 'Master, let me receive my sight.' And Jesus said to him, 'Go your way; your faith has made you well.' And immediately he received his sight and followed him on the way.[7]

This is how it works – by revelation, insight and praxis. This is the paradigm of discipleship; you see, and you take the Way.

Religion takes what is spiritual, interior and manifested, reinterpreting it as material, exterior and controlled. It creates a confusion between appearance and reality. You can see this very vividly in the Franciscan movement. It starts with St Francis of Assisi, rebuilding a (literal, physical) ruined church with his own hands, inspiring followers, begging for his food and squatting in a disused donkey shed. Such a path resists formalization, so once the movement begins to harden into an institution, things have to change. Brother Elias is elected as Minister General of the order at the General Chapter of 1232, and the wandering tradition is abandoned in favour of residences, study centres and organized communities. The Rule and the distinctive habit, for all the beauty of the Franciscan order, cannot ever capture and systematize the living flame of St Francis. And those who follow in the way of St Francis can be seen but will never be recognized, because that's how it was with the little poor man

---

7 Mark 10.49–52 RSV

of Assisi – like Jesus, he was of no account and people thought he was crazy. Once you leave that behind in favour of a sensible, practical and organized establishment, you can have something admirable and worthwhile and highly effective – but it won't be Francis. The way of St Francis might or might not be there in the life of any given Franciscan.

The difficulty is that if you choose the new and living Way, you lay down the security of position, status, recognition and power. You can't accredit or establish or institutionalize it, because that isn't possible. If you take that way, there is grace and providence and the sublime refuge of love, but there is no establishment, no house, no salary, and you can't make a name for yourself. It is a way of smallness and insignificance. Not only does the Lord *require* nothing of you but to do justly, love mercy and walk humbly with thy God, he doesn't *offer* you any more than that either. This runs counter to our natural instinct to colonize and to establish power bases that goes with the frail nakedness of our physical humanity with its hairless skin and large brain. From the moment we set foot on the new and living Way until the moment it takes us into glory, we are never for a instant free of the yearning to stop and settle down:

> Jesus took with him Peter and James and John his brother, and led them up a high mountain apart. And he was transfigured before them, and his face shone like the sun, and his garments became white as light. And behold, there appeared to them Moses and Elijah, talking with him. And Peter said to Jesus, 'Lord, it is well that we are here; if you wish, I will make three booths here, one for you and one for Moses and one for Elijah.' He was still speaking, when lo, a bright cloud overshadowed them, and a voice from the cloud said, 'This is my beloved Son, with whom I am well pleased; listen to him.'[8]

---

8   Matthew 17.1–5 RSV

Therefore let us go forth to him outside the camp, and bear the abuse he endured. For here we have no lasting city, but we seek the city which is to come.[9]

The Way of Jesus is written in the Book and can be traced in the lives of the Ancestors, but it cannot be captured; it can only be lived, because it is itself alive. It cannot be formalized because it is always new:

And Moses said to them, 'It is the bread which the Lord has given you to eat. This is what the Lord has commanded: "Gather of it, every man of you, as much as he can eat; you shall take an omer apiece, according to the number of the persons whom each of you has in his tent."' And the people of Israel did so; they gathered, some more, some less. But when they measured it with an omer, he that gathered much had nothing over, and he that gathered little had no lack; each gathered according to what he could eat. And Moses said to them, 'Let no man leave any of it till the morning.' But they did not listen to Moses; some left part of it till the morning, and it bred worms and became foul; and Moses was angry with them. Morning by morning they gathered it, each as much as he could eat; but when the sun grew hot, it melted.[10]

Attempts to formalize and define the Way are perennial, but they serve only Mammon, not God, because, as Jesus explained[11], you can't do both.

The question then naturally arises, are not the organized religions of the world the channel for a huge amount of good? Surely it takes

---

9   Hebrews 13.13-14 RSV

10 Exodus 16.15-21 RSV

11 Matthew 6.24

systems and mechanisms, rules and paid staff, to run charities for the relief of famine and orphanages for children whose parents have died of AIDS and hospitals and schools and refuges for victims of domestic violence? All these things the Church does. To be effectively kind and to focus generosity usefully, don't we need a system?

Undoubtedly yes. The problem is not that organizations and institutions exist, nor that the Church is one of them. Where things go wrong is when the external machine itself is confused with the goodness it was intended to channel. The zeal that properly belongs to bringing healing and mercy to troubled situations, to working for peace and justice and the wellbeing of creation, is commonly misapplied to developing and maintaining the structure intended to carry these good things. The result of this misapplied zeal is indistinguishable from perfect cynicism. No doubt the Bible is a holy and inspired book, but the church that takes verses from it as proof texts to conduct witch hunts, with a view to burning at the stake those who can be caught out by them, has turned itself into a monster.

Organizations and institutions, rules and systems, even creeds and catechisms, are easy to police and enforce, whereas simple goodness is not. It's a lot easier to determine whether someone has a certificate or has broken a rule than to assess if they are gentle and humble and kind. It's more straightforward to exclude someone because they are female than because they are spiteful or lazy or lecherous. The trial of Joan of Arc is a perfect example of this. That she was honest and holy, brave and sincere, did no more for her than make it hard for her inquisitors to convict her. That her prison guards repeatedly tried to rape her did not disturb the Christian leaders who brought her to trial. But that she was wearing trousers and that she was a virgin (they checked) was of immense importance. And the trousers were the main reason they burned her alive. To my mind, burning someone alive because they are wearing trousers is everything that is wrong with organized religion crystallized into one moment in time. It poisons all the intended goodness of the institution's working. Of what use are the orphanages if they are hellholes where little children are sexually abused? Of what use is the missionary if he is the harbinger of shame and oppression? Of what use is the church that fundraises for victims of war when at the same time it blesses the troops and the bombers and turns a blind eye to the arms fairs?

The confusion between (or imaginative conflation of) the religion of Christianity with the new and living Way of Jesus has led to inappropriately channeled zeal. So people get zealous about others keeping rules, rather than about the life of prayer or the way of love.

This is only exacerbated by the confusion, in Enlightenment thinking, between the inside and the outside. The mechanistic view of living beings that developed with the eighteenth-century Enlightenment exaltation of scientific method enhanced the tendency to attribute insides to ourselves while seeing everyone else as outsides – so, we have feelings, but they have behaviours. This quickly manifests as ruthlessness – the screams of hurt animals are 'vocalisations', fear and suffering no longer evoke pity, knowledge and authority are given sovereignty and compassion is dismissed.

The new and living Way as it affects women and men

It's one thing to find fault with present systems, but that can't help us unless we have something to put in their place. Our difficulty is, as Albert Einstein pointed out, 'We cannot solve our problems with the same thinking we used when we created them.'

I see this in the Church's Safeguarding systems, put in place to protect children and vulnerable adults from systematic abuse within the institution of the Church. Heavy-handed and cumbersome, legalistic and punitive, at best intensifying complication and creating requirements that make hospitality and mercy unworkable in many real settings, and at worst exacerbating the problem by chasing out predatory individuals to the margins, from where they dip in and out of the community life of the Church on a casual basis, unchecked. Systems, rules and institutions offer the perfect setting for opportunistic predation. Secrecy, authority and hierarchy create the perfect scenario for covering the tracks of injustice and cruelty.

In respect of Safeguarding, where the questions were asked, 'What helped? Where were children safe?' it quickly became clear that children were protected not by stiff policing of predators, but by adults listening to children and taking them seriously. What helped was restoring agency to children – for instance, giving them choice when it came to establishing boundaries, not insisting they allow adult family members to kiss and cuddle them in rituals of greeting. It helped when children knew their concerns would be heard: in instances when adults had time to listen, when the child's voice counted. In such scenarios, the predators *policed themselves*; abusers refrained from abuse because they could not ensure it would go undetected where adults listened to children.

So, what can we realistically do to allow the new and living Way of Christ to appear in the Church that was intended to promote it? How can we allow the sacred gospel to continue to be written in our daily lives? What will allow men and women to flourish and be happy alongside one another?

First, Christian discipleship absolutely requires simplicity. It is not possible to travel this way encumbered with baggage – this path demands too much focus, involves too much responsibility. It asks each pilgrim to do the interior soul work necessary to become a lightning rod of God's power. The pilgrim has to be paying attention, be available, flexible and free to wait upon God. Though the connection with gender roles is not immediately obvious, this is a prerequisite for putting things right. The person who is burdened with complexities, duties, commitments, social engagements and possessions does not have room inside to question assumptions and habits of mind deeply enough. Old tracks and stock responses claim the one who is tired and over-committed. Unless we concentrate (in the fullest sense of the word) and bring all the power of our intelligence to this task, we just end up channeling the Ancestors and maintaining the status quo. To move on, we must travel light, and to do that we must adopt a discipline of simplicity. It is essential.

A discipline of simplicity advantages women even more powerfully than it advantages men. In a global society where the gender bias with corresponding financial advantage is still heavily in favour of men (for varied and complex reasons), high-maintenance women still in general rely on manipulating men and being sexually attractive to men in order to achieve the symbiosis guaranteeing their financial security – keeping them housed, fed, clothed, educated and (where necessary) medicated. As the old saying goes, 'The one who pays the piper calls the tune.' Practitioners of simplicity, minimalism and essentialism obtain significant freedom from existing systems, which acts most in favour of those who benefited least from the system – women.

So the first task is to obtain the clarity that simplicity brings, availing ourselves of the silence and solitude we will have won.

The next task is forgiveness. There is so much history to this issue, and it is so shocking, so violent and so unjust, that we cannot hope to get the apologies and reparations we might feel were appropriate. Part of our moving into the discipline of simplicity will involve facing and dealing with the shame and grief, the fear and resentment, the uncertainty, as we prepare to lay aside accustomed privilege or servitude; for all this is baggage too heavy to carry. Setting it aside is a decision, yet not carried out in a short space of time. You have to keep skimming away the dross as it rises to the surface. You need the humility to continually step back, begin again, see mistakes forming.

Allowing ourselves to start with a clean slate is important – no debts owed for the past, no grudges borne – but no quarter given, either, for continuing the oppression and exclusion of women. This is no longer negotiable. It has to stop.

Then it is helpful to consider how male and female energies work in group negotiation. There is, of course, significant variation according to personality and skill level, and it's worth taking into account the apparently increasing phenomenon of neurological difference; a person with ADHD or who is on the autistic spectrum may not communicate and negotiate as you expect. But in general, masculine energies are characterized by the sword, and feminine energies are characterized by the cauldron.

Sword energy is dominating and hierarchical – a top-down energy, seeking a leader, a chain of authority, and a set of rules. It groups people into serried ranks like an army facing a commanding figure at the front, or like a pointy pyramid with a bee of inferiors holding up the commanding apex. It looks for obedience, expects compliance, seeks to find a place in a chain of command, and its stress response is fight-or-flight. It protects (by violence), but it also wounds. It instils fear. It coerces. It speaks of heroes, warriors, battles, enemies, strongholds, kingship, victory and defeat, taking sides – familiar vocabulary in the Church.

Cauldron energy groups everyone in equidistance around the central empty negotiating space. Each one is important, none more than any other – the grandmother, the baby, the breadwinner, the teenager, the pregnant woman; all are of equal importance, though each one's needs and contribution will be unique. Cauldron energy manifests in listening, in holding space for one another, in coming to a common mind. It expects to compromise and to be patient; it values helping one another. Its stress response is tend-and-befriend.

In social history, Gandhi's ashram was a very interesting blend of sword and cauldron energy. Gandhi used the sword energy of his cultural background to cut out a space for cauldron energy to begin. If you look at Gandhi superficially, he appears to have been a natural leader of great assurance and conviction. It's always worth digging deeper, though. As a child, he was timid and fearful, frightened of many things – ghosts, the dark, all sorts of shadowy threats. His strength developed in overcoming fear. Gandhi was not naturally fearless but habitually brave. His courage made him a force to be reckoned with. As a Hindu man, he expected and assumed loyalty and obedience from his wife. So it came about in his ashram, when Kasturbai (Gandhi's wife) baulked at his edict that every member would clean the toilets – no Dalits here – Gandhi simply ordered her to comply. This is sword energy in action, assuming and pulling rank, and it was deeply ingrained in him from his cultural upbringing. Yet he was using it to put in place a community where cauldron energy could appear, everyone equal and all contributing, each one serving and helping and no one lower in status than the others. Because sword energy cuts through and takes charge, it does have the virtue of getting things done with despatch. Cauldron energy isn't *better* than sword energy; they're just different.

Because sword energy cuts and conquers, it tends to scatter cauldron energy – make it disappear. A good example of this in the Bible is Paul insisting that the women be quiet in church. Why? To maintain order, so they can listen to the leader, the speaker. That's sword energy; everyone in silent, respectful ranks listening to one person who sticks up above the crowd, more important and more senior than they are. Paul is using his sword to scatter the cauldron energy of women listening to one another, discussing, sharing, not paying respectful attention to one man standing at the front being important. In today's congregations, café church has begun to manifest cauldron energy in public worship: sitting round tables, everyone listening and everyone contributing. Historically, Quaker worship has been our best example.

An important aspect of cauldron energy is the element of choice inherent in every voice being heard and every contribution valued. Choice has many benefits. It switches on our mental powers of initiative and evaluation and wakes up our interest in what's happening. Just having to do as we're told makes us dull and unresponsive; the word schoolchildren use for it is 'bored'. Choice turns on our creative power and stimulates our subconscious mind. Choice involves us, increasing our commitment to group process. It also has a surprisingly healing effect physically as well as mentally (because all aspects of our being are linked). Giving choice to residents in geriatric care homes – small choices, such as 'Would you like a pot plant in your room? Yes? Which of these two colours would you like?' – has been shown to improve urinary continence. And choice helps to keep people safe; if a child doesn't have to attend the children's group run by the adult of whom they are afraid, if they have the choice to say 'No' about food and touch and clothing and playmates, they are strengthened against abuse.

Cauldron energy also protects through the power of many witnesses. Secrecy is much valued in church tradition, and gossip is denigrated as shameful. But grapevine communication, sharing of what we have observed, checking the responses of those we trust, helps deepen understanding and insight, makes us aware of danger, keeps us safe. Within the circle of community, women and children are safer than when they are separated and isolated. All round the world, women often choose to have a companion with them – when they go to the market, to the doctor, to the temple or out in the fields.

Making church a safe space for women and making wider society a safe space for women should be high on our agenda. Rape culture[12] has prevailed for far too long. Cauldron energy can help us turn the ship.

In the Christian communion, we have the two potent images of the cross and the chalice. The cross looks like a sword and is a symbol of overcoming, conquering, victory, enemy defeated. The

---

12 This is a huge topic of its own, about which such an immense and accumulating amount has been written in recent years that I am assuming the reader understands I am referencing the worldwide social tendency to exploit and commodify women rather than simply the specific criminal occurrence of what the law courts technically describe as rape.

imagery connected with the chalice, cup of blood, has been distinctly under-explored.

Looking at our models of faith community to notice where we can see sword energy and where cauldron energy, in our vocabulary and ways of being together, will help us move towards a communion that feels safe and affirming for everyone in it. Cauldron energy resists oppression.

If we are to invite an inclusive church to take shape, we will do well to work in the idiom of the circle. This can be a challenge for the traditional preacher: 'Where will I put my notes, how will I stand so everyone can see and hear me? Where is the front? How will I manage without a lectern and a podium?' We can quickly see that our whole way of doing and being church is challenged by the image of the circle.

Symbolism and imagery have latent power; they are not merely decorative, and changing the symbolism with which we express our faith is not gimmicky tinkering with tried and true tradition. The Judaeo-Christian tradition has been strongly patriarchal in both its praxis and its imagery. How we express our faith in language and image is a way to start humming a new tune without conflict or confrontation. Our church fathers and the men who shaped our tradition have given us a beautiful, precious, strong witness. They have taught us and nourished us. But it is also true that women have lived with oppression and subservience in the Church and at times have been cruelly vilified and persecuted only for being female. Gently, without drawing binary battle lines or allowing a pendulum swing that now vilifies men, let us make our praxis more spacious, so that everybody's voice can be heard. This is not to say that lifting the curse of Eve from our church communities can be a process characterized entirely by sweetness and light. In a world where docility and subservience has been expected of women – where they are present to decorate, serve and please – women who speak directly and hold their heads up straight will initially be experienced as culturally jarring, intimidating and argumentative, while men who are gentle will either be unduly congratulated or regarded as weak. But we can use our intelligence and the vast expanse of information available to us to educate ourselves, to push through this and to create justice.

We know that the large institutions and organized hierarchies of sword energy consistently work to the disadvantage of women[13] – their top-down structure and incremental accumulation of advantage or disadvantage ensures this. Families and informal networks where trust and familiarity are the means to success (rather than formal accreditation and promotion), the sphere of cauldron energy, are the settings where women have traditionally found the means for security and creativity[14]. Yet, where the institution opens its eyes to the power of cauldron energy, working actively towards inclusiveness rather than domination, we can change the status quo of inevitable male privilege. And where a family is toxic and the cauldron cooks up something poisonous, in such circumstances, the sword energy of the formal institution can cut through and rescue. It's not 'either/or' but 'both/and' that we need.

The creation blessing of Genesis 1 – 'In the image of God . . . male and female he created them. And God blessed them . . .'[15] – is of male and female *together* in the image of God, the cauldron and the sword working together to balance and harmonize: what Taoism calls Yin and Yang, forces that are not opposing but complementary, the breathing in and breathing out of creation, the rhythm of love.

---

13 See the careful and systematic work of Virginia Valian in her book *Why So Slow? The Advancement of Women*, MIT Press; New Ed edition (26 Feb. 1999), ISBN-10: 0262720310, ISBN-13: 978-0262720311.

14 For instance, in my own family, a line of strong women has used resources to good advantage, but this remains hidden because it has been done informally; there is no means of recognition. But recognition is a value of sword energy; security rather than recognition is the objective of cauldron energy, and that's what we've created in our family.

15 Genesis 1.27-28 RSV

Before we finish . . .

let's reflect

1 The cross and the chalice are very powerful symbols of our lives in the faith of Christ. What do they mean for you? Spend a little while quietly with each image and jot down what the cross means to you . . . and what the chalice means to you . . . Was it easier to relate to one image rather than the other? If it was, why might that be?

2 The sword and the cauldron are old representations of masculine and feminine energies. How do you respond to them? Spend a little while quietly with each image and jot down what the sword means to you . . . and what the cauldron means to you . . . Was it easier to relate to one image rather than the other? If it was, why might that be?

3 Thinking about your responses to the cross and to the sword – how are they similar and how are they different? Thinking about your responses to the chalice and to the cauldron – how are they similar and how are they different?

4 Spend a little while thinking about your own spiritual path – the road you have travelled and where you are now. What would be a fitting spiritual symbol to represent this?

5 What are your feelings about how men and women find their place in the family of faith, their roles and contribution? Do you feel all is well with this, or are there aspects that make you feel uncomfortable? Is there anything needing healing? Is there anything that should change? If there is, how do you feel we might best approach these things?

6 How do you feel about the physical layout of our churches and the vocabulary we use in worship? In what ways do these things affect our discipleship? Can you think of a place you have been that really helped you to worship? What was it like? Can you think of a song, or a service you went to, where the words drew

you into a deeper experience of God? Are there any changes you would love to see in your own fellowship's patterns of worship?

7 What has helped and what has hindered your growth as a Christian?

We can never expect perfection of ourselves and each other. It is not easy or straightforward to cast off old ways of doing things and the settled cultural habits of millennia. No doubt there will be struggle and misunderstanding as we continue to work towards a truly inclusive and healing expression of church. But let us never be discouraged. Surely we can trust that what Christ petitioned for will come to pass, and he prayed:

> Father, the hour has come; glorify thy Son that the Son may glorify thee, since thou hast given him power over all flesh, to give eternal life to all whom thou hast given him. . . . And now I am no more in the world, but they are in the world, and I am coming to thee. Holy Father, keep them in thy name, which thou hast given me, that they may be one, even as we are one.[16]

May it be so.

---

16 John 17.1,11 RSV

WE HAVE A VISION OF A WORLD IN WHICH EVERYONE IS TRANSFORMED BY CHRISTIAN KNOWLEDGE

As well as being an award-winning publisher, SPCK is the oldest Anglican mission agency in the world.

Our mission is to lead the way in creating books and resources that help everyone to make sense of faith.

Will you partner with us to put good books into the hands of prisoners, great assemblies in front of schoolchildren and reach out to people who have not yet been touched by the Christian faith?

To donate, please visit www.spckpublishing.co.uk/donate or call our friendly fundraising team on 020 7592 3900.

An easy way to get
to know the Bible

'For those who've been putting aside two years in later life to read the Bible from cover to cover, the good news is: the most important bits are here.' Jeremy Vine, BBC Radio 2

The Bible is full of dramatic stories that have made it the world's bestselling book. But whoever has time to read it all from cover to cover? Now here's a way of getting to know the Bible without having to read every chapter and verse.

No summary, no paraphrase, no commentary: just the Bible's own story in the Bible's own words.

'What an amazing concept! This compelling, concise, slimmed-down Scripture is a must for anyone who finds those sixty-six books a tad daunting.'
Paul Kerensa, comedian and script writer

'A great introduction to the main stories in the Bible and it helps you to see how they fit together. It would be great to give as a gift.'
Five-star review on Amazon

The One Hour Bible
978 0 281 07964 3 • £4.99